PUBLIC SPEAKING

The Self Help Guide to Mastering Small Talk,
Presentations and Influence in Communication

(Boost Your Overall Networking Skills and Become
a Leader)

Nancy Reynolds

Published by Rob Miles

© **Nancy Reynolds**

All Rights Reserved

Public Speaking: The Self Help Guide to Mastering Small Talk, Presentations and Influence in Communication (Boost Your Overall Networking Skills and Become a Leader)

ISBN 978-1-989990-14-8

All rights reserved. No part of this guide may be reproduced in any form without permission in writing from the publisher except in the case of brief quotations embodied in critical articles or reviews.

Legal & Disclaimer

The information contained in this book is not designed to replace or take the place of any form of medicine or professional medical advice. The information in this book has been provided for educational and entertainment purposes only.

The information contained in this book has been compiled from sources deemed reliable, and it is accurate to the best of the Author's knowledge; however, the Author cannot guarantee its accuracy and validity and cannot be held liable for any errors or omissions. Changes are periodically made to this book. You must consult your doctor or get professional medical advice before using any of the suggested remedies, techniques, or information in this book.

Upon using the information contained in this book, you agree to hold harmless the Author from and against any damages, costs, and expenses, including any legal fees potentially resulting from the application of any of the information provided by this guide. This disclaimer applies to any damages or injury caused by the use and application, whether directly or indirectly, of any advice or information presented, whether for breach of contract, tort, negligence, personal injury, criminal intent, or under any other cause of action.

You agree to accept all risks of using the information presented inside this book. You need to consult a professional medical practitioner in order to ensure you are both able and healthy enough to participate in this program.

Table of Contents

INTRODUCTION 1

CHAPTER 1: BUILDING YOUR CONFIDENCE INSIDE OUT 5

CHAPTER 2: MAKING YOUR LIFE BETTER THROUGH EXPRESSION 13

CHAPTER 3: WHAT IS CREATIVE VISUALIZATION? 26

CHAPTER 4: WHY ARE YOU HERE? 31

CHAPTER 5: EMPOWERED LEADERSHIP 39

CHAPTER 6: THE AUDIENCE- KNOW THEM 44

CHAPTER 7: HOW TO FEEL CONFIDENT IN FRONT OF YOUR AUDIENCE 47

CHAPTER 8: HOW TO SPEAK IN PUBLIC 59

CHAPTER 9: THE PHYSIOLOGY OF PUBLIC SPEAKING 67

CHAPTER 10: FEARLESSNESS THEN WHY AM I SHAKING? 79

CHAPTER 11: BENEFITS OF BECOMING AN ACE PRESENTER AND WHY GIVING A GREAT PRESENTATION MATTERS 92

CHAPTER 12: SIGNS OF PUBLIC SPEAKING FEARS AND ANXIETIES 102

CHAPTER 13: PUBLIC SPEAKING AND SPEECH ANXIETY . 108

CHAPTER 14: AUDIENCE PARTICIPATION 115

CHAPTER 15: SO YOU DON'T LIKE YOUR AUDIENCE? 120

CHAPTER 16: KNOW YOUR AUDIENCE 129

CHAPTER 17: LOOK AND FEEL CONFIDENT 133

CHAPTER 18: UNDERSTANDING WORD POWER 140

CHAPTER 19: LEARNING FROM FAMOUS PUBLIC SPEAKERS 153

CHAPTER 20: WHAT IS PUBLIC SPEAKING 157

CHAPTER 21: PROFESSIONAL PUBLIC SPEAKERS 169

CHAPTER 22: THE SAME CONFERENCE BUT DIFFERENT PEOPLE 175

CONCLUSION 182

Introduction

I know why you are reading this book...because you want to learn once and for all the secrets on how to master public speaking and overcome your fears of public speaking! (Or perhaps you know someone with this challenge and you would love to help!)

Well you have taken the first step in solving this problem! You have already identified that you have a problem that needs a solution. You are willing to open your mind to the solution that will help you over time. You have recognized that you have the fear of public speaking and you just want to get over it!

You have simply chosen the right book at this time in your life!

What you will get from this book is a lifelong way of developing your public speaking skills in a practical manner that will grow as you grow.

As a Public Speaking coach for the better part of twenty years, teaching teens, adults, in the corporate world, at the university level, in workshops, it is really remarkable to see how widespread the fear of speaking in public is! It is remarkable to me because it is not a fear I really had the chance of having.

I started doing drama in high school – so I was forced to speak in public at a very early age, 11 years old, in my first year. I had the chance to speak in public as another character, so yes, I still hid behind another persona, but still I was speaking publicly. I am still doing theatre after thirty years, but additionally I am a broadcaster for over 25 years, but still behind a microphone, so still had the opportunity to do some hiding.

Once when I was emceeing a show with a fellow broadcaster, he admitted to me that he did not like public speaking, it is his number one fear, like so many others. I also learnt that public speaking is feared even more than death!

The experiences in broadcasting and theatre helped honed my skill as a speaker – but not necessarily as a public speaker- I had to learn on my own. I had to develop my own voice, why? Because I had opinions to share, jokes to give, compliments to give and inspirational stories to tell.

You too have opinions to share, ideas to present, jokes to give, compliments to give, inspirational stories to tell, toasts to give and presentations to make. You want to win at public speaking! You don't want it to be just a one-time thing, but you want to be able to do it, each and every time, without butterflies in your stomach, with bold confidence and to great applause.

It is a pleasure for me to be a public speaker, to be able to share comfortably with an audience, no matter the nationality of the audience, the age group, educational level, the venue or anything, for that matter, I am always ready!

I want to share my ideas with you, but you must dedicate at least six weeks to retraining yourself in the art and science of public speaking to ensure that you grow as a public speaker. Do each and every exercise – I promise it will take you over the top as you become a witty, confident speaker.

Be alert in reading the book, as throughout the book you will learn specifically how to overcome the particular fears you may have about public speaking.

Chapter 1: Building Your Confidence Inside Out

In my early years, I used to think that confidence was something that could be given to me. I remember thinking that if I was dressing in a certain way, or perhaps if I owned a certain item I would feel cool. Or maybe if I was friends with some of the most popular kids in school, I would become more confident like them. This kind of thinking was because I felt that my confidence was dependent on other people's acceptance of me. I had this crazy idea that if somehow people accepted me, I would become more confident. In fact, I will become more.

However, the truth is that the absence of confidence has little or nothing to do with the perception of others. Yes, it is possible that the opinions and cruel words of other people can erode your confidence, but even that is done with your own permission. The main issue at the heart of the matter is this simple fact; the absence of confidence in a person comes from their inability to accept themselves for who they are.

Confident people don't wear the coolest clothes. They don't have the latest gadgets. As a matter of fact, some of the most confident people I know are not even wealthy. They are just regular Joes, doing the regular thing and just being themselves. To build your confidence, you have to first generate personal acceptance. Our inability to accept ourselves for who we are is sometimes tied to things that we perceive as flaws. When we meet people, we think that these perceived flaws are on display and this makes us feel vulnerable. We all know that the more vulnerable we feel, the less confident we are.

Vulnerability is something that we share in an intimate environment and when you are in public, the circumstances are less than intimate. So, it is understandable why you wouldn't feel confident in that moment. To deal with that, you would need to build your confidence and arm yourself with inner strength to the point that the vulnerability you experience on stage will not overwhelm and overshadow your speaking capacity. We are going to be looking at five things you can do now to build your confidence.

1. Love Yourself

Building your confidence is a process that's going to have to start from the inside of you. You need to accept yourself for who you are. I remember something one of my teachers was fond of saying. She was a huge fan of Whitney Houston and often said, "You can't spend your life waiting for someone to love you and if you don't love yourself you can't expect someone else to love you because the greatest love of all is inside of you". If you are the type of person who has spent a lot of time criticizing parts of yourself, you are going to have to invest more time undoing the damage you have done. Things like positive affirmations, positive self-image and general positive thinking might be able to help you reverse the damage.

2. Do Something

The next step in this process is to actively participate in the transformation of yourself. And to do that, you first have to ask yourself, what are those things that make you feel uncomfortable? The common complaints I hear people have about themselves have to do with weight issues or a specific part of the appearance generally. Then you also have people who have speech defects. Later in the book I will touch on this briefly, but in the meantime, what you can do is to take actions that will help you get over your dislike or in approval of yourself. For instance, if you feel that you are overweight, you can start a weight loss plan. As for physical appearances, besides undergoing a surgical procedure to correct it, you may want to learn ways to enhance or disguise those features. In my opinion, I think that sometimes the problem is that, we focus too much on the flaw and ignore, or rather refuse to see the beauty in our imperfections. For speech defects and similar issues, talk to a speech therapist. Steve Harvey was known to have a speech defect. He had a bad stutter. Today, he runs one of the biggest talk shows.

3. Be Adventurous

Many of us are sleeping in our comfort zones and the moment we are taken out of these zones, we feel vulnerable. These repeated patterns creates a cycle that leads us to a point where there is a complete lack of confidence in ourselves. To break this, you need to challenge yourself. Get up every day and do something that you have never done before. You don't have to go big right away. Little changes to your daily routine can give you a sense of adventure. Something as simple as changing the type of coffee you have every morning can help you take the necessary steps to becoming more confident. The key is building on this as you go.

4. Set Yourself Up for Success

When it comes to fashion, the style gurus will tell you that "perception is everything". If you are able to style yourself and look like you came out from the pages of a fashion magazine, good for you. But this is not about what you wear, rather how it makes you feel when you wear it. True style comes from your own interpretation of your personality. This goes on to feed your confidence. You could be wearing the latest trends from the biggest designers, but if this is not a reflection of who you are on the inside, you would not be confident on the outside. Just ensure that you are obeying the basic fashion rules such as dressing for the occasion. So, go ahead and dress to impress. But remember, the number one person who should be most impressed is you.

5. Brace Yourself for Impact

Life is not a bed of roses. This is a common phrase but it's wrong. Life is indeed a bed of roses because you have the flowers, the leaves and then you have the thorns. Harboring the illusion that you are going to walk out and do everything on this list and people are going to accept you and love you can be devastating when you find out otherwise. So, brace yourself for those thorns. Remind yourself that there are people out there who take delight in tearing other people down. It has nothing to do with you but it has everything to do with them. Those words or actions can sting but, they don't cause any real damage unless you dwell on them. Think of yourself as oil and their words as water they can only get you on the surface but there's no way they can penetrate the center where it matters.

Growing your confidence can take a while. Don't expect to snap your fingers and become confident overnight. You would need to be deliberate, consistent and patient with yourself.

Task:

Take a sheet of paper and in three words, write out three things you like about yourself physically, emotionally and socially. Beside each quality, write out why they stand out for you. Example;

Physically: Thick, long hair. I can style it in different ways

The words you use to describe these qualities must be positive.

Chapter 2: Making Your Life Better Through Expression

When you are able to speak effectively in public, your whole life improves. It gives you greater confidence, success, and a feeling of accomplishment. You will gain personally when you speak well because you will be able to articulate your story and feel as though you are being understood. You will gain professionally because employers seek and promote employees who can communicate well. -You will benefit by being more engaged in your community by feeling confident about engaging yourself in civic life. The three main benefits of learning to publically speak are personal, professional, and civically.

PERSONALLY:

Think about how gratifying it is when you are able to tell a story about yourself in a convincing and an articulate way. It feels good to tell people about yourself in a way that uniquely describes who you are. It is great to be able to develop what I call a "This is my story" speech – a compelling, personal narrative that expresses who you are in a way no one else can tell.

PROFESSIONALLY:

I challenge you to look on an employment Web Site or in an employment section of a newspaper and find jobs that DON'T ask for effective communication skills as a requirement for the job. Employers seek employees who can present themselves well, speak on their feet, and motivate students through their speech.

CIVICALLY:

You don't know how you will speak out in your community. What if your child needs learning initiatives not offered by your school district? With the skills you'll gain in this class you will feel confident about speaking about your needs – perhaps helping those in your community—and your own child in the process. Maybe you would like to speak to a civic group about your passion or your work (or maybe if you are lucky, your passion is your work).

Effective speech will help you speak in the community with passion and eloquence.

When you stand up and speak for something, perhaps in a way you never imagined, or when you identify a need for utterance, you are encountering a rhetorical situation. In history there have been many occasions for rhetorical situations: President Reagan addressing the nation after the Challenger Disaster; President Bush addressing the nation after 9/11; President Obama addressing the nation after the school shootings in Newtown, Ct. But you don't have to be the president to speak in response to a rhetorical situation. After their 19-year-old daughter Jeanne Clery was murdered on her college campus by a fellow student, her parents, Howard and Constance Clery, mounted a campaign for campus safety. The result is the Jeanne Clery Disclosure of Campus Security Policy and Campus Crime

Statistics Act. Mr. and Mrs. Clery did not expect to speak out about campus security, but their tragedy caused them to respond rhetorically so that campuses would be safer throughout the United States. [1]

The Origins of the term the Rhetorical Situation

Communication scholar Lloyd F. Bitzer described the concept of the rhetorical situation in his essay of the same name. [2] The concept relies on understanding a moment called "exigence," in which something happens, or fails to happen, that compels one to speak out. For example, if the local school board fires a popular principal, a sympathetic parent might then be compelled to take the microphone at the meeting and/or write a letter to the editor. Bitzer defined the rhetorical situation as the "complex of persons, events, objects, and relations presenting an actual or potential exigence, which can be completely or partially removed if discourse, introduced into the situation, can so constrain human decision or action as to bring about the significant modification of the exigence."

Some elements of the rhetorical situation include:

Exigence: What happens or fails to happen? Why is one compelled to speak out?

Persons: Who is involved in the exigence and what roles do they play?

Relations: What are the relationships, especially the differences in power, between the persons involved?

Location: Where is the site of discourse? e.g. a podium, newspaper, web page, etc.

Speaker: Who is compelled to speak or write?

Audience: Who does the speaker address and why?

Method: How does the speaker choose to address the audience?

Institutions: What are the rules of the game surrounding/constraining numbers 1 through 7.

Analyzing the rhetorical situation (at its most fundamental, means identifying the elements above) can tell us much about speakers, their situations, and their persuasive intentions.

The ancient Greeks gave special attention to timing--the "when" of the rhetorical situation. They called this **kairos**, and it identifies the combination of the "right" moment to speak and the "right" way (or proportion) to speak. Let's get back to the school board example. After voting to fire the popular principal, the sympathetic parent might grab the microphone and scream invectives at the board. This would be bad **kairos**. Perhaps a better choice would be to recognize that a mild rebuke fits the situation followed by a well-timed letter to the editor or column in the school newsletter.

Public Speaking is Both Ancient and Modern

Public speaking is both a very old and a very new form of expression. The way we think of contemporary public speaking—at least the Western tradition of public speaking—is based on the works of the ancient Greeks and Romans who forged an especially insightful system of rhetoric or public speaking. This tradition has been enriched by the experiments, surveys, field studies, and historical studies that have been done since then. Every day in colleges and universities around the world scholars of speech communication and rhetoric are advancing the knowledge about effective public speaking through new studies of speakers (known as rhetors) and the circumstances that surround their speeches. All of this research extends the groundwork of knowledge about rhetoric that was begun by ancient Greek scholars.

Aristotle's Rhetoric, written some 2,300 years ago, was one of the earliest systematic studies of public speaking. It was in this work that the three kinds of proof—logos (or logical proof), pathos (emotional appeals), and ethos (appeals based on the character of the speaker)—were introduced. This three-part division is still followed today.

Roman rhetoricians added to the work of the Greeks. Quintilian, who taught in Rome during the first century, built an entire educational system—from childhood through adulthood—based on the development of the effective and responsible orator. Throughout these 2,300 years, the study of public speaking has grown and developed. Contemporary public speaking builds on this classical heritage and also incorporates insights from ~~the~~ humanities, ~~the~~ social and behavioral sciences, and now, computer science and technology. Likewise, perspectives from different cultures are being integrated into our present study of public speaking.

A Greek term of interest here is **agora** – or the public forum. Once you develop your public speaking skills, you will be eager to enter a public forum and share them – whether that public forum is at the local Rotary meeting or on the World Wide Web as a TED talk, building your public speaking skills helps you share your message with the greater audience.

You may be thinking: all of this background about public speaking is interesting and you can see the benefits of becoming a successful speaker, but how do you actually improve your skills?

By reading this book, thinking about your feelings about public speaking, and by practicing your skills every chance you get, your public speaking skills will improve.

In her best-selling book: **Quiet: The Power of Introverts In a World That Can't Stop Talking**, Susan Cain makes an important distinction that introverts can be very effective public speakers. Most people think that all good public speakers are naturally outgoing extroverts. That isn't true. Both introverts and extroverts can be effective public speakers. The terms introversion and extroversion were first popularized by Carl Jung. Extraversion tends to manifest itself in outgoing, energetic, talkative behavior. Introversion is manifested in more reserved, quiet and shy behavior.

There are several factors that figure in to your success in developing your public speaking skills:

Natural Talents

Education and Training

Practice

Natural Talents:

Consider how you 'feel' about public speaking. Are you eager to do it any time the opportunity arises? Or, are you more like former Supreme Court Justice Sandra Day O'Connor who, when I asked her if she likes public speaking, replied, "I don't mind it."[3] Or, would you like the title of a public speaking how-to book to say, "I'd rather die than give a speech"[4]! Your answer to that question may be a good idea where you think you fall on the 'natural talents' scale. Usually if people think that they are naturally good public speakers, they very much enjoy it and are eager to do it. But even if you would "rather die", you can be an excellent speaker with education and practice. So please, hang in there!

Education and Training:

There's a lot of education and training to help you become a better public speaker. You are taking a course and reading a book that are getting you some excellent education and training right now. In addition to traditional college courses, you could join a Toastmaster's Group, or simply read all the material you can get your hands on about effective speech. Watching speakers on YouTube, in person, and on television is another great way to improve your understanding of what makes a good (and not so good) speech.

Practice:

This might be the best predictor of your success in public speaking than natural talent and education and training. If you are willing to put in the time to speak and hone your skills, you will improve. It takes repetition and patience, but it is the surest path to success. I interviewed former Kansas senator and presidential nominee Bob Dole and he told me he and his senate colleagues never practiced their public speaking. "It is why we aren't any good," he said wryly. On the other hand, he added, his wife, former North Carolina senator and presidential candidate Elizabeth Dole, "practices a speech she's going to give even if she's given it twenty-five times before."[5] That's why throughout her career, Elizabeth Dole has been lauded for her extraordinary public speaking skills. Practice makes you better, and often makes you great.

Finally, as you think about your public speaking needs, consider the purpose of the speeches you are about to give. In other words, why are you speaking? Speech purposes include:

To inform

To persuade

To entertain

To celebrate

Chapter 3: What Is Creative Visualization?

Creative visualization is a mental or psychological technique that is used to create a positive mental picture that will influence and guide your life. In other words, it is a technique that allows you to accomplish your desires with the use of your imagination.

A famous verse in the Bible goes like this: "As a man thinks in his heart, so is he." The concept of creative visualization is very much the same, and as you can see, it is not necessarily a new concept or a new idea.

So if it isn't so new, why is there a need to read about creative visualization and know more about it? Why is it essential to practice it? Can't we just immerse ourselves in positive thoughts all the time? As you may already know, life is not easy. Even at a very young age, people from various walks of life may experience pain, suffering, sadness, loneliness and failures.

These negative experiences affect a person's confidence, self-esteem, sense of reassurance and optimism. A single traumatic experience can lead a person to lose hope, become mistrustful and insecure. We are surrounded with negative issues every single day. Even news reports give us more bad and worrisome news than inspiring ones. This is why subconsciously; our minds are filled with fears and doubts, even when we try to be optimistic. It is for this reason that creative visualization is essential to instill a sense of optimism both consciously and subconsciously.

In new thought psychology, creative visualization is largely linked to the **law of attraction**, which simply states "like attracts like." This means that a person who focuses on positive thoughts are likely to attract positive people, positive experiences and positive outcomes, pretty much in the same way that a person who dwells on negative thoughts will attract negative people and negative outcomes.

To help you further understand what creative visualization is all about, here are some descriptions about this concept:

1. Creative visualization involves positive thinking. Since creative visualization also uses the tenets of the laws of attraction, you will be trained to keep positive thoughts and sensations in mind whenever you are engaged in the creative visualization process.

2. Creative visualization is about confidence. Creative visualization techniques are geared towards developing your confidence in terms of goal achievement and social relationship success. It gives you knowledge and assurance of positive outcomes as a result of thoughts and visualizations that detail how these outcomes are achieved.

3. It gives empowerment. What logically goes with confidence is empowerment. Creative visualization removes the limits to

what you can do and achieve. Since it helps remove your negative thoughts and ideas, you will be empowered to take more risks, take more action and make more initiatives. The statement changes from asking "Can I do it?" to knowing that "I can do it."

4. It encourages perseverance. Creative visualization encourages perseverance rooted in self-belief. No matter what life throws at you, you will learn to grasp the truth that you have the power to shape and change various situations to make them pleasant and agreeable.

5. It is planning. There is a reason that this process is called **creative visualization,** and not just visualization. Creative visualization techniques enable you to plan scenarios in your mind that will produce your anticipated results. This means you have to use your different senses, your knowledge on a variety of issues and all other information available to you in order to visualize successfully.

6. Creative visualization is influence. Remember the law of attraction mentioned earlier? The quality of your thoughts attracts the types of people, experiences and situations that will come to your life. In this sense, creative visualization is influence. You get to select the areas of your life that will have a hold or influence on your way of thinking, acting, behaving and ultimately, living. This will have a similar effect on the people you deal with – those who draw near to you will radiate the same kind of mental attitude that you have learned to adapt – positive, unbeatable and remarkably successful.

Creative visualization will change your way of thinking and living. Although its techniques will not require you to adopt a certain spiritual or metaphysical level or belief, it does entail the use of an open mind that does not limit or set boundaries to your capacity to achieve.

Chapter 4: Why Are You Here?

Picture this.

It is the day before your big presentation. The big boss and his team are coming over from head office and they are bringing the biggest company client to hear what your project will do for them. No pressure then. You are leading the project of course but you just handle the boring bits like the figures and plans while Mike does the exciting work on design. Mike was not told to present, was he? You were. Part of your ongoing professional development. What did your boss say to you? Oh yes, "Great leaders are always great speakers" or something similar. It is not like you have not done this before though is it? There was the one in Belgium in front of the accounts department and it went OK. Well you knew them all of course and it was only facts and figure for 10 minutes which was as easy as falling off a log. This, however, is a world away at forty-five minutes presenting to a big crowd of heavy hitters you do not even know.

Good grief!

Do you have your slides ready and in the right order? Do you have back-up copies in various formats? Do you have flip chart drawings prepared to match your card notes in case it all goes wrong and the projector breaks? Are you anywhere near prepared enough?

Are your slides too boring? Do you think two hundred and fifty slides chock full of bullet points, figures and charts will be enough for forty-five minutes? Will you freeze and forget your lines? Will you stumble and stutter your way through it all?

No sleep for you tonight then.

Bet you cannot wait for the upset stomach tomorrow or the sweating and shaking before you go on. Will you remember your lines? What will your audience think of you? Will they see you shaking and quaking? Will your mumbled apologies and requests for some slack to be cut go unheeded? Are they there to see you die on your backside as the saying goes?

The thought of speaking in public has reduced you to a nervous and shambling wreck.

Does this seem all too familiar to you? We have all been there – even the great speakers. In fact, some of the great speakers may have been even worse and worked harder to overcome it or turn it to their advantage.

Many people experience nerves prior to speaking in public.

Some people experience outright terror in this situation.

How are you with public speaking nerves?

The scenario most people picture when thinking about public speaking is the speech in front of a large audience. However, speaking in public covers many other situations such as presenting an annual conference report, training other people, speaking up or presenting at a meeting, attending an interview and many more could easily be listed here.

If you do suffer from nerves prior to speaking out loud in public, then rest assured you are not alone. To paraphrase and expand on Mark Twain's famous quip; "There are only two types of public speaker in the world - those who admit to getting nervous and the liars who say they don't."

*Every public speaker feels nerves. Experienced speakers may get nervous for different reasons than beginners, but all speakers get nerves of some kind.

A certain level of *nervousness is generally a healthy thing and indicates a natural desire to do well. The general adrenaline rush of pre-talk excitement can also be misinterpreted as nerves and you need a balanced perspective of the situation and how to handle it. These pre-event nerves can be relatively easily handled yourself or, shameless plug alert, with the help of a personal speaker coach, such as my good self, if you prefer.

As the sub-title of this book states, to reduce your public speaking nerves you must acknowledge them, understand them and accept them to gain control over them and even use them to your advantage. You also must begin with and maintain useful and effective mindsets to realise your full potential as a speaker. This short practical no-nonsense guide will help you get there.

If you are an expert who speaks then you can always be an expert who speaks better.

So, stress not, valued reader. You will get all the theory and practical information you will need to first understand and then to more confidently manage and deal with public speaking and presenting nerves as well as understand and manipulate your mindset and attitude toward speaking in front of others. You will start to build the confidence to spread your wings and become a far better public speaker, presenter and communicator.

Each chapter builds your knowledge and many feature end of chapter "Action points" to encourage you to take a practical and proactive approach to trying out the techniques and ideas. Live practice and solid feedback are the only ways to get good at something.

The first half of the guide looks at nerves and how to control them and the second half focuses more on the speaking mindset aspect. You will find your mindset also has an enormous impact on controlling nerves. As you will no doubt have noticed, I have made a deliberate and specific decision to make sure this book is laser-focused and flab free. I appreciate your valuable time is at a premium so with that in mind I am making my books only as long as they absolutely need to be to get the message out there and doing good things.

My coaching clients all benefit from short intense sessions, so I have chosen to create all my "How To …" practical guides to closely replicate this short yet intense experience in book form. Each book in the series is self-contained and each fully delivers on its promise. They are all effectively equivalent to five or six hours of one to one coaching with me distilled into the written word. The series will aim to offer a comprehensive system of learning for the avid reader.

As I mentioned above, this volume is aimed primarily at experts who speak in public. Experts who speak, be they leaders, managers, technicians, engineers, salespeople, entrepreneurs, coaches, trainers or indeed any other expert you can name, generally seek to become experts who speak better rather than expert speakers. In my experience they seek to find an accessible, practical and no-nonsense solution to their problem and this is where my guide fits in.

I hope you enjoy and benefit from this guide and, if you have not already done so, please check out and enjoy my many other books and guides.

By the way, I am constantly building a portfolio of high quality training audios and on-line video courses related to mental toughness, resilience, emotional intelligence, mindfulness and business management/communication skills so please get in touch if there is one you would like me to create and I will consider it. Check out the current list on my Amazon author page or my website.

*Please note, if you are particularly terrified or phobic about public speaking (it is technically known as glossophobia) to the extent to which it is adversely affecting many aspects of your work and personal life, rest assured it can be overcome but you will need to invest in some more specialised one to one speaker coaching along with confidence building sessions from someone, such as my good self, who is highly experienced in this field.

Chapter 5: Empowered Leadership

No more does a one size fits all leadership model truly work. We can't treat everybody the same and expect that everything will just "work out" someway. Managers and leaders must have a framework with which to manage their workers in a way that honors everyone's unique and particular position on the job. Empowered leadership is the way to do just that. Empowered leadership shares the power between management and the workers, thus empowering both groups. Conventional knowledge tells us that when those in power relinquish that power by sharing it or giving it to their employees, then they would lose something when truly, they gain something.

Think about it. When individuals rule with an iron hand, they typically instill fear in those who work for them. Do you do your greatest work whenever you are frightened? I don't know about you but I will try to comply simply because I want to steer clear of negative consequences but it certainly won't be my greatest work. The absolute greatest a manager could hope for with coercion is compliance. If compliance is enough, then coercion may work.

Nonetheless, I will gripe and grumble and quietly wait for opportunities to get even. I won't have a kind thing to say about my employer and at every accessible chance will seek corroboration for how I feel from my co-workers, thus spreading an "us" versus "them" mentality. When leaders and managers seek to empower their workers, they will gain their loyalty. Workers want to give their supervisor their greatest when they're listened to and respected. Without fear, their minds could be creative and innovative.

When managers are willing to accommodate particular requests and it doesn't interfere with product or service delivery, then their employees will be sure to give back their greatest in return. Giving away power only raises a manager's power.

Now, I am not talking about being a total pushover and only advocating for what employees want. As a manager, you have a two-fold job-you are to represent your employees' desires, opinions and suggestions to management whilst all at once communicating management's issues, concerns and expectations to your employees. This is not an uncomplicated line to walk. You will never get the greatest from your employees if they don't respect you. You can not be a doormat for your employees to walk over. If they believe you've got no bottom line or nonnegotiables, then they will never be satisfied and always asking for more. You will feel used and abused and the truth is, you asked for it. As a manager, you must hold the bar high. Expect fantastic things from each and every one of your workers. If you only expect mediocrity, mediocrity is precisely what you will get. Set the standards and lead by example. In case your workers see you giving it your all, it's going to be challenging for them to perform beneath standard.

You must have production goals you are attempting to meet for either products or services. Always enlist the help of your employees to set the goals, with the underlying premise being continual improvement.

And as a manager, you have the obligation to create a need satisfying workplace for your self and your workers. You can not emphasize one to the exclusion of the other without there being unwanted consequences.

Whenever you concentrate on production only and forget the human capital, you will end up with resentful, resistant, annoyed workers. On the other hand, whenever you only concentrate on the people end and let production goals to be compromised; you will have workers who do everything they could to take advantage and to get out of doing the work. After all, if you the manager don't value production, why should they? Someplace in the middle, whenever you are walking that really fine line between relationships and production goals, you are practicing empowered leadership and that's where you will get the most from your employees.

Chapter 6: The Audience- Know Them

Who is your audience? It is important to know who they are before you begin preparing your speech. If it is a group of people in a retirement home, you would not be wise preparing a speech on the "Practical Methods of Skateboarding". If you were in high school, you would not be interested in a speech on "How to Really Love Your Grandchildren". They would not be interested. It would not be practical and you would be wasting your time. By the same token, a well executed speech on the subject of "Understanding the Medicare Prescription Drug Plan" would be something most of the senior adults would be interested in, and yes, the high school students would be more interested in skateboarding. They would listen, and you would be an instant success.

Determine who you are speaking to and gear your speech with them in mind.

As we think about the audience, we need to realize that knowing them (who they are) and getting to know them personally will be a great asset in the success of your presentation. Someone wisely said, "They don't care what you know until they know that you care."This applies to all speaking situations. Whoever you will be speaking to will be a better audience if they know that they are important to you and that you really are concerned for their well being. In addition, if you will get to know them it will help you set yourself at ease- more on that in a future chapter.

I like to get to the place I am speaking early, before the audience gets there, just to get the feel of the place. This helps me to feel more connected with the audience. When the audience arrives, I get to know as many of them as I can. I kind of evaluate the situation and know a little about their culture. This is far better than walking on to the stage at the last minute and starting the speech. My audience is very important. I must have their ear and their heart. This is a vital part of getting them to accept what I am saying to them.

Chapter 7: How To Feel Confident In Front Of Your Audience

The fear of public speaking is one of the top fears that people have. Statistics show that over 41% of people have some level of fear or anxiety with regards to speaking in front of an audience. This fear often manifests as excessive sweating, sweaty palms, increased heart rates, blanking out (memory loss), nausea and sometimes difficulty breathing. There are many speakers who have been in front of audiences for years and they still deal with anxiety to some degree.

Since having this fear often has no bearing on whether you have to do a presentation or not, you'll have to find some ways to overcome your anxiety. The first step is to know that you are not alone and that you can prepare in advance so that the level of fear you feel is significantly reduced. Here are some other interesting statistics.

- Proper presentation and rehearsal of your message can reduce your fear by about 75%.

- Utilizing breathing techniques can reduce your anxiety by another 15%.

- Preparing for your mental state can reduce your fear the remaining 10%.

With these statistics in mind, here are some preparation tips to help you relax and reduce how you feel before going in front of your audience.

1. Know the environment you will speak in. Become familiar with the area by arriving early and walking around. Know how much space you have and the physical distance between you and your audience. As you acclimate yourself to your stage, you will find yourself feeling more comfortable.

2. Know your audience. You should find out who comprises your audience and do some research to find out their likes and dislikes. When they enter the room, greet

them and take time to get to know some faces.

3. Know your presentation inside and out. If you don't know what you'll be presenting how can you expect yourself to feel fearless?

4. Implement breathing techniques to help you relax. Breathing techniques have been scientifically proven to invigorate the body and help you get rid of nervousness.

5. See yourself on stage before you actually get there. Replay images of your successful presentation in your mind. If you visual success, you'll find it.

6. Know that your audience wants you to succeed. Your success means they get what they want and need. If they've paid money to attend your presentation, they have a personal stake in your success. If you're providing training, they have a personal stake in your success. If you're delivering a graduation speech at a local university, the graduating class has a

personal stake. Get the idea? Your audience wants you to succeed.

7. Don't draw attention to your being nervous. Many people won't even realize that you are nervous. Most times you will find that while you have your audience's attention, they are really thinking about themselves. They are absorbing what you say and processing that into how that relates to them.

8. Know that there is a purpose to your message. You have a message to deliver. Sometimes it's a cause that you are passionate about. Other times, it may be training that your company needs you to give.

Preparation is the key to your success! Through preparation, you can also overcome most if not all of the feelings of fear that you might have so prepare, prepare, prepare!

A Professional Speaker Sets The Tone For The Message

As a professional speaker, everything you do the minute you walk into the room sets the tone for your message. Without even speaking one word, you can determine just how many people you will reach because their engagement to your message depends on you; not on them. You can have a great topic to speak on and great presentation skills, but without communication the passion you have about your topic, none of it really matters!

Go before your audience expecting to make an impact! People aren't interested in what you know. They want your information for themselves and passion is like the "grease" that lubricates that passage of information! Do you expect that your audience will receive what you have to say? Do you communicate that you're excited to be there and you're also excited that they are there as well?

Be mindful of the needs of your audience. As a professional speaker, we can get caught up with our message because you know it's what your audience needs. The problem with that train of thought is that it leaves one key person out of the equation - your audience member. Prepare yourself beforehand to figure out what your audience may want to know or needs to know and then deliver that message.

Change things up for maximum impact! There are going to be times when you can't stay stuck to your outline. Learn to improvise and adjust to the needs of your audience. Find ways to engage them as you proceed throughout your message. Do you remember in school that one teacher you had that you could never seem to connect with? Students were falling asleep in class and the teacher still plodded on with their message! How effective is that? Change your presentation and tailor it to engage your audience no matter where they might be! Don't stay stuck in a routine!

Relate to your audience. Relating to your audience goes beyond just speaking to them. It encompasses everything from the greeting you give, the way you dress and your tone of voice you use to address them. Part of relating to your audience means knowing who they are and what appeals to them. You'll have to research beforehand who your audience members are. If you do this, you'll be positioning yourself to be more relatable to them.

Passion is the key that opens their hearts and minds to receive what you have to say! If you're passionate about your topic, that will come across in your speech by default. Conversely, if you lack passion about your topic, that too will also come across. Do you really believe in what you're talking about? Do you see the value that you and your message have to offer your audience? When you practice your speech, do you motivate yourself? Just about every professional speaker starts off practicing by looking at themselves in the mirror! Try doing that and take a good look at what you see!

You are the key to a successful delivery of your message. If you want to see results, understand that you set the tone in your meeting and it's up to you to maintain control of that tone!

Give Them A Bit Of You

There is a good reason that public speaking is a superior method of presenting material to a group than just faxing your text over and letting them read it. Yes, part of that reason is that by stepping through the talk, you can make sure they "get it". But the most important reason has to do not with the subject, not with the presentation style and not even with how good the donuts were before talk. The reason public speaking is so effective is that the audience gets the material presented in a very personal way by the one person who can do that - you.

When people walk away from your talk, they will remember one thing as their primary memory and another level as secondary. The secondary memory will be your subject matter. But the most potent memory they will carry with them will be that of you as a speaker. Public speaking is actually a very personal thing to your audience. That is because while to you, you are speaking one to many, to each audience member, you are talking to him or her directly. That bond is unspoken but strong. And it is even stronger when you address the same crowd regularly.

This may seem like an awesome responsibility but buried in this little fact about public speaking is a secret to make your presentations more effective. Instead of shying away from the fact that people will feel like they know you after you address them in a public, embrace that fact of life about speaking in public and use it to your advantage. The way to grab a hold on this powerful psychological principle is simply to give them more of you in every aspect of your talk.

You can start with your introduction. Its easy to tell some joke you heard on the late night talk shows and then go right into your talk. But if you take a moment and speak to them person to person, you will create a stronger bond with them which will result in better results from your presentation. Take some time and reveal a little bit about yourself to this group. Public speaking can be a very cathartic event because when you open up to a group of people about your feelings and your past, they embrace you emotionally and that presentation becomes personal to them.

But don't stop adding the personal touch with the introduction. Continue to look for ways to make the presentation personal throughout the talk. You no doubt know the power of illustrations, stories and humor in any presentation. Well instead of using abstract or canned stories or jokes, personalize this aspect of your talk. Don't just 'tell a joke". Instead think of a personal story that has a humorous component to it and use that to illustrate the point. By using humor that makes fun of you, not only will the laughter be more genuine, it will ingratiate you to the crowd and create that connection between the personal speaker/audience bond to your subject matter.

The same is true of illustrations. Now there have been cases where speakers made up a personal story to fit the talk so that is done. And because it has the same effect, you could put that under the category of "acting" and not feel to badly about it. But if you use a real story from your own life, your childhood or your love life, that will ring true during your talk and be more believable to your audience.

Don't be intimidated by putting some of your own heart and life into your public speaking. The investment of giving people a little more of you will result in a higher level of concentration and responses to your call to action. And the audience will emotionally bond to you in such a way that you will almost certainly be asked back to speak again and again.

Chapter 8: How To Speak In Public

There are two essential qualifications for making an effective public speech.
First, having something worth-while to say, and secondly, knowing how to say it.
The first qualification implies a judicious choice of subject and the most thorough preparation. It means that the speaker has carefully gathered together the best available material, and has to familiarize himself with his subject that he knows more about it than anyone else in his audience.
It is in this requirement of thorough preparation that many public speakers are deficient. They do not realize the need for this painstaking preliminary work, and hence they frequently stand before an audience with little information of value to impart to their hearers.
The second essential of an effective public speech is knowing how to say it. This implies a thorough training in the

technique of speech. There should be a well-cultivated voice, of adequate volume, brilliancy, and carrying quality. There should be ample training in articulation, pronunciation, expression, and gesture. These so-called mechanics should be developed until they become an unconscious part of the speaker's style.

Your best opportunity for practice is in your everyday conversation. There you are constantly making speeches on a small scale. Public speaking of the best modern type is simply elevated conversation. I do not mean elevated in pitch, but in the sense of being launched upon a higher level of thought and with greater intensity than that is usually called for by ordinary conversation.

In conversation you have your best opportunity for developing your public speaking style. Indeed, you are there, despite yourself forming habits, which will disclose themselves in your public speaking. As you speak in your daily conversation you will largely speak when you stand before an audience.

You will therefore see the importance of care in your daily speech. There should be a fastidious choice of words, care in pronunciation and articulation, and the mouth well opened so that the words may come out wholly through the mouth and not partly through the nose. Culture of conversation is to be recommended for its own sake, since everyone must speak in private if not in public.

One of the best plans for self-culture in speaking, is to read aloud for a few minutes every day from a book of well-selected speeches. There are numerous compilations of the kind admirably suited to this purpose. The important thing here is to read in speaking style, not in what is termed, reading style as what is usually taught in schools. When you practise in this way it would be good to imagine an audience before you and to render the speech as if emanating from your own mind. The student of public speaking will wisely guard himself against acquiring an artificial style or other mannerism.

Another good plan is to make short mental speeches while walking. When possible it is well to choose a country road for this purpose, or a park, or some other place where one's mind is not likely to be often diverted by passers-by. Lord Dufferin, the eminent British orator, was accustomed to prepare most of his speeches while riding on horseback. The habit of forming mental speeches is a great aid to actual speech-making, as it tends to give the mind a power and an adaptability, which it would not otherwise have.

Three Pillars of Public Speaking

 Ethos Pathos Logos

Written in the 4th century B.C. the Greek philosopher Aristotle compiled his thoughts on the art of rhetoric. Aristotle wrote down the secret to being a persuasive speaker, the secret which forms the basis for nearly every public speaking book written since then.

Ethos: credibility (or character) of the speaker.

Pathos: emotional connection to the audience.

Logos: logical argument.

Together, they are the three persuasive appeals. In other words, these are the three essential qualities that your speech or presentation must have before your audience will accept your message.

Ethos or the ethical appeal means to convince an audience of the author's credibility or character.

An author would use ethos to show to his audience that he is a credible source and is worth listening to. Ethos is the Greek word for "character." The word "ethic" is derived from ethos.

Before you can convince an audience to accept anything you say, they have to accept you as credible. Ethos is your level of credibility as perceived by your audience.

There are many aspects to building your credibility:

Does the audience respect you?

Does the audience believe you are of good character?

Does the audience believe you are generally trustworthy?

Does the audience believe you are an authority on this topic?

Pathos or the emotional appeal means to persuade an audience by appealing to their emotions. Speakers use pathos to invoke sympathy from an audience; to make the audience feel what the author wants them to feel. A common use of pathos would be to draw pity from an audience. Another use of pathos would be to inspire anger from an audience; perhaps in order to prompt action. Pathos is the Greek word for both "suffering" and "experience." The words empathy and pathetic are derived from pathos.

Do your words evoke feelings of … love? … Sympathy? … Fear?

Do your visuals evoke feelings of compassion? … Envy?

Does your characterization of the competition evoke feelings of hate? Contempt?

Emotional connection can be created in many ways by a speaker, perhaps most notably by stories. Pathos can be developed by using meaningful language, emotional tone, emotion evoking examples, stories of emotional events, and implied meanings.

Logos or the appeal to logic means to convince an audience by use of logic or reason. To use logos would be to cite facts and statistics, historical and literal analogies, and citing certain authorities on a subject. Logos is the Greek word for "word," however the true definition goes beyond that, and can be most closely described as "the word or that by which the inward thought is expressed, Latin.

Oratio; and, the inward thought itself, Latin Ratio. The word "logic" is derived from logos.

Logos is synonymous with a logical argument.

Does your message make sense?

Is your message based on facts, statistics, and evidence?

Will your call-to-action lead to the desired outcome that you promise?

Logos can be developed by using advanced, theoretical or abstract language, citing facts (very important), using historical and literal analogies, and by constructing logical arguments.

Chapter 9: The Physiology Of Public Speaking

In my particular case, I found considerable solace in gaining an understanding of the neurobiological processes which underpinned my fear. For some reason, knowing that I felt a particular way due to a range of common brain processes gave me comfort. Now, whenever I feel a particular type of anxiety due to whatever reason, I quietly say inside my head "Ah, there is my amygdala tagging something as fearful". Some people feel that their fear and anxiety makes them "crazy", subject to some unimaginable process alien to others. An understanding of what is happening "under the hood" can be extremely helpful in my experience. I will therefore dedicate some space to explaining exactly what is going on inside your head when you are fearful of public speaking.

If an alien landed on Earth and you told him (or **her**, or **it**) that 75% of all humans, when talking to a group of other humans, experience intense fear (despite no threat of bodily harm), the alien would (perhaps quite rightly) think humans were insane. And to some extent the alien would be correct. When you think about it, the idea that standing in front of people and talking would cause you to panic (as if you were under attack) is bizarre.

A great way to illustrate the sheer lunacy of this fear is by again describing an aspect of my own **glossophobia** (the official term for the fear of public speaking). I am someone who has no problems talking to people. I am quite social and often the centre of attention, comfortably talking to large groups of my friends at dinner parties or in an office context. If you told me I had to explain a topic to a stranger or a co-worker I would have no problems. If you added another person so that I was explaining the concept or topic to two people I would feel no anxiety. However, if you kept adding people, at some point (I never knew the exact number of people which was my own tipping point) my brain would decide that I had crossed the threshold from just "talking to people" to "presenting to a group of people". At some indeterminate point, my brain suddenly seemed to think it was in danger! Another aspect of my own personal insanity was how much notice I was given before I was required to present. Again, one particular incident perfectly illustrates this also. One day in the office I was minding my own business when a senior manager of the company I worked for suddenly emerged from a meeting room near my desk and beckoned for me to come in. I walked into the room to find the entire senior management team assembled in front of me, whereupon I was promptly asked to explain a research project I had been working on with no notice (or ability to prepare). As my brain had had no time to fret anxiously about this impromptu speaking engagement, I just started talking extemporaneously and felt little (if any) anxiety. If this particular presentation had been requested a week earlier, I would have experienced a week of misery and would have been in a state of near-petrification in the moments leading up to it.

To reiterate – anxiety is a strange beast that can often operate seemingly without rhyme nor reason.

In his paper The Biology of Fear and Anxiety-Related Behaviors, Thierry Steimer expertly describes anxiety thus –

Now, if we were to slice open the brain to locate the source of this bizarre behaviour, we would find the prime (but not only) culprit buried deep in the temporal lobe. The name of this culprit is the amygdala (or amygdalae), an almond-shaped organ (or more specifically, a cluster of nuclei). The amygdala is often referred to as your "fear centre", however this can be a little misleading as it appears to indicate that the amygdala is just involved in fear or negative emotions. Whilst the amygdala is central to your fear reaction, it is also one of the parts of your brain that give life its colour and emotion. The amygdala is the first line of defence in **attaching emotional significance to events**. People with impaired amygdala function (due to brain injury or other reasons) live a life devoid of emotion. By all accounts it is an awful existence. It seems that the price we pay for intense emotional joy is the propensity to feel equally intense negative mind-states such as anxiety.

The reason why the amygdala appears to act illogically is that the amygdala acts in a way that neuroscientists refer to as "quick and dirty". The best example of this is the often-used snake/rope example.

Say you are walking through the forest or jungle and out of the corner of your eyes you glimpse a coiled object on the ground. Typically what will happen is, before you know it, you have jumped back, stress hormones coursing through your veins. Then, moments later, you realise that it was just a coiled length of rope, not a snake. You can thank your old buddy the amygdala for this.

What has just happened is that your amygdala has made a snap judgement based on very rough, low-resolution information. Your amygdala literally says "I'm not sure whether that is a snake or just an innocuous snake-like object, however just to be safe I am going to initiate panic stations". The reason why this process is called "quick and dirty" is that it bypasses the logical, reasoning part of your brain and hijacks your brain and body, based on very rough information. Meanwhile, the signal has also gone from your eyes, through your brain's relay station and eventually arrived at your conscious, thinking brain, moments after the amygdala has already done its work. This is the point where your logical brain, armed with a hi-resolution image from your eyes, decides that you are looking at a piece of rope and are therefore in no danger.

So, why does the amygdala have such a propensity for overreaction? Because, over the course of your ancestor's evolution, an overactive amygdala has kept everyone safe. Sure, an overactive amygdala has caused countless false alarms and often made things psychologically uncomfortable, but an underactive amygdala would quickly thin out your gene pool. Put another way, the costs of panicking at the site of coiled rope (or snake-shaped vines, for example) are mild, whereas the costs of not jumping back quickly when there actually **is** a deadly snake, can be massive.

In general, the way the amygdala works in this context is that there is a particular event which the amygdala then **tags** as something important. There was a fantastic experiment some years ago which perfectly illustrated how the amygdala works (apart from the fact that this experiment sounds, on the surface, a little cruel).

This experiment was conducted on a person who had a severe memory problem which meant they were unable to remember anything. So if a researcher came into the room and introduced themselves to this person, left and then came back in, this poor lady would have no memory of every having met the researcher. Then the researcher tried something interesting. They put a small drawing pin in their palm so that when they shook hands with this lady it gave her a small prick, causing her hand to recoil. The researcher then repeated this several times. Then something fascinating occurred. Despite the fact that she had no ability to remember the researcher, eventually, when the researcher offered to shake hands the lady didn't want to shake hands for some reason and could offer no reason as to why. This was because, whilst her typical memory centre was not functioning, her amygdala retained the ability to tag certain events as significant.

So eventually her amygdala knew that there was something about shaking hands with this person that was potentially dangerous.

Herein lies one of the major problems with the amygdala and the reason for almost every single possible phobia. Firstly, the amygdala often makes mistakes, tagging something as dangerous when it is perfectly innocuous. This can lead to illogical phobias such as the fear of public speaking or a fear of heights (where you are in no actual danger, yet feel intense anxiety nonetheless). Secondly, once the amygdala has made up its mind about something, it is extremely difficult and time consuming to extinguish the fear. This is why exposure therapy takes so long to work. Say you are afraid of snakes. First you need to imagine the snake, then you need to look at pictures of snakes, then you need to look at videos of snakes, then you need to look at real snakes in the zoo, until hopefully you reach the point where you can physically handle a non-venomous snake. Each of these stages can take months for severe cases. Essentially what you are doing in this scenario is gradually, ever so slowly, trying to convince the amygdala that snakes present little actual danger.

Whilst the amygdala plays a central role in the fear response that underpins your public speaking anxiety, it is by no means the only part of the brain involved. There is actually a complex network of connections between various parts of your brain that becomes activated by certain stimuli (such as standing up in front of people and presenting). The chief neurotransmitter used to communicate messages around this network when you are stressed or aroused is norepinephrine (or noradrenaline in some countries).

The main sub-group of this network is known as the hypothalamic pituitary adrenal axis (HPA axis). When you are physiologically aroused by a stressful stimulus, a message is sent along this axis, involving the release of adrenaline and cortisol to prepare you for fight or flight. Your body essentially prepares itself to both run away quickly (by liberating blood glucose and fatty acids for energy) and repair itself (by ramping up the inflammatory process).

Finally, another part of the brain, known as the **locus** ceruleus (sometimes spelled coeruleus) is also implicated in the fear response and particularly, the panic response. Your locus ceruleus is your brain's major factory for norepinephrine. When you are subjected to fear-provoking stimuli, your locus ceruleus lights up and dumps norepinephrine into your brain to be used for arousal-related signalling. Drugs such as benzodiazepines and barbiturates work to some degree by dampening the activity of the locus ceruleus by increasing levels of the calming neurotransmitter GABA (gamma amino butyric acid), which puts the brakes on your locus ceruleus.

Apologies if I have bored you to tears with all this neuroscience, however I believe it is vital to understand exactly what is going on at a biological level. Your reaction to public speaking is not unique. You are not alone. And the biological process that is occurring in your brain is happening due to ancient fear structures over which you have little conscious control.

Chapter 10: Fearlessness Then Why Am I Shaking?

The same things that we fear are the same things that give us confidence when we overcome them. That's why you'll find this section on fear and the next section on confidence so closely related.

One of the first fears you have to get over, if you haven't already, is looking people in the eye.

I can't tell you how many times I have seen speakers who can't make eye contact for even half a second as they prance from one set of eyes to another. Or they skirt their eyes over their audience's heads rather than look at them. If you have improvement to make in this area, start developing that eye contact in everyday conversations with friends, family, co-workers or acquaintances. You will soon feel more comfortable making eye contact with everyone you meet, including your audience.

Looking people in the eye, not staring, but looking them in the eye, tells people you are confident and sincere. The other plus is, when you look your audience in the eye they are less apt to tune you out. It draws people in to pay closer attention to what you are saying. Good eye contact is essential.

Second, have you ever said to yourself: "I **can't** do this. I'm going to look stupid" or "Oh no, oh no, I'm having brain freeze, I can't even remember my first line let alone my first word." Th-a-a-a-t was me when I started in acting. I would get on stage, find myself trembling with fear and get so anxious that I would go totally blank. Plus, I would have to go to the bathroom one hundred and one times before getting to the stage. I know, I know, TMI.

Or how about this scenario? You are at home rehearsing, you do such a great job, express yourself so freely, you can be dramatic, funny … You ROCK at home … by yourself.

Do you do that when rehearsing a speech? Do great at home and then crumble when you have to face an audience? I did too.

When I first started out acting, I was so frightened that I had no connection between what I was thinking, expressing outwardly or truly feeling. I was what you'd call "ONE HOT MESS." You want to know a little secret? Deep down inside I had a DESIRE to be fearless, to conquer those fears. It was that desire that drove me.

Do you have that DESIRE of fearlessness in you? Then "Feed on the desire, not on the fear." Let your desire drive you. The only way we can make that desire come alive in us is to continue to step out of our comfort zone and FEED on the DESIRE.

When I transitioned into public speaking, it had been at least 12 years since I had done any acting. It took me two months before I worked up the nerve to do my first speech in a Toastmasters club. It wasn't as nerve-wracking as when I started acting—yet all those old fears welled up in me. I made every excuse in the book for the first two months. Especially the biggest ones, "I'm not ready. I need more time." Yep, I was trying to be perfect. Are you trying to be perfect?

You're not going to be perfect now or ever.

How long are you going to say, "I'm not ready, I need more time"? You're not going to be perfect now or ever. Change that, "I'm not ready," to "I can do this, I will do this." And say it out loud. Yes, even I have to remind myself to say that at times. Let yourself hear yourself say it.

Once you do that first speech in front of an audience, you will begin to feel a little more confident. You'll never be ready if you don't take that first step. "Feed on the desire, not the fear."

Continue to rehearse, rehearse, rehearse; do, do, do; refine, refine, refine then rehearse it again, do it again and refine it again. But always remember what Tami Evans said, "Personality and passion trump perfection."

When you rehearse a speech, you are exploring the possibilities and they are forever evolving.

You may be asking why I said to "rehearse" your speech instead of practice it. When you rehearse a speech you are exploring the possibilities and they are forever evolving. You'll begin to see practice as practicing the technical parts of a speech, **i.e.**, knowing you have to pick up a prop, cross to a certain part of the stage, use your clicker for a power point. We practice the technical to make it look natural within the rehearsal process.

Keep observing and learning, seek out advice from those whose abilities you seem to connect with.

Third, let's talk about visualization; I'm a big believer in this. There have been studies done on successful people and one of the common factors was they could see themselves where they are at today when they were just starting out.

Here are four steps to help you:

1. First, without spoken words … take the time to visualize yourself doing your speech. Visualize the room, the audience, see yourself walking the stage, but most important see yourself doing a great job delivering your speech.

2. Second, rehearse your speech out loud at your normal speaking level, but this time, talk to that statue, that picture, that light switch in your living room. Make those inanimate objects your audience. Look at THEM as if they have eyes and are

looking back at you. And YES, visualize the reactions you are getting.

3. Third, when rehearsing out loud even if you mess up or go totally blank, visualize your audience looking at you, all right staring at you, all eyes are on you; what do you do? Panic, right? Wrong!

Here are some suggestions to help you. Repeating the last line or word you said can sometimes help trigger you to get back on track. Or, you might use a little humor by saying something to your audience like this, "I forgot my next point and I was worried about my 90-year-old mother forgetting things." Maybe you address your audience this way, "I've just lost my train of thought, what was the last thing I said?" I've seen high profile speakers do that. Here's where you picture the audience smiling and replying back to you, helping you out. Audiences love to help you, because they want you to be successful; otherwise they wouldn't waste their time coming to listen to you.

Get yourself to the recovery room and continue with your speech.

4. Which brings me to point four. Don't EVER, EVER apologize for forgetting a line or losing your place. If you do, you've just drawn more attention to the mistake and made it a negative. The audience will remember the negative which makes it even harder for you to recover. In contrast if you make it a positive, laugh at yourself, get the audience to laugh with you, get them to help you ... by the time you finish your presentation, the audience will have forgotten a mistake ever happened. Or, if you move on to the next thought the audience won't ever miss what they didn't know you were going to say. Easier said than done, right? It's natural for us to want to apologize when we mess up, but we have to learn to move on. Our minds race so fast ... we're giving our speech, reading our audience, thinking about what comes next, then kicking ourselves because we forgot an important word or

point; we have a lot on our minds, don't we?

The most important thing is the way you handle it. And yes, things sure feel different when you face a live audience. But how you prepare for them and the way you handle a situation is what will make the difference.

Remember, the audience wants you to succeed.

Come with me now and let's look in on a seminar on public speaking I attended a few years back. This has a couple important points I want you to grasp.

There we were sitting in the audience ready to gain some important knowledge on public speaking from a so-called "professional speaker," let's call her Liz. Liz began and ended her presentation pacing back and forth, back and forth, back and forth across the floor. Let me ask you, do you remember one important thing she said? Probably not, because you got so caught up in her continual pacing back and forth. Too much movement distracts and detracts. Then a question and answer period came, and someone asked her, "How do you control nervousness?" She answered, "I drink coffee." She wasn't kidding either, she actually said, "That's what I do, I drink coffee." If you were me you would have jumped out of your chair and screamed, "NOOOooooo," but you're not me and you believe her. No, no, no, no, no, no, no.

Not only was it bad advice, but it was pretty obvious she drank coffee considering she barely stayed in one spot for more than one second; she walked on every important point, thus making those points negligible. Coffee is one of the worst things you can drink before speaking—it doesn't CALM your nerves, it's a stimulant, plus the caffeine dries out your throat and mouth. You have to ask yourself, how is it people like her get paid to speak? And I confess, I asked myself that very question.

…as you learn and grow, don't believe everything you hear.

This is one reason it is important to recognize that as you learn and grow, don't believe everything you hear. Ask questions, learn what others do. Coffee is not the answer; make good choices, make it your own and then add it to the stage you are building for yourself.

The other point in this story was the fact that the speaker not only walked continually but she walked on every important point. When you walk on important points, people are watching you move, not listening to what you say. This brings me back to the advice I got from the gentleman earlier. His movements didn't flow during transitions; they were abrupt and looked rehearsed as he moved robotically around the stage. This also became a distraction. Two different scenarios, yet two examples of ineffective speaking.

Lastly, one of the most basic things you can do to help calm your nerves is to take a few deep diaphragmatic breaths before going on stage. We will go through the Breathing Exercise in Chapter 6.

You are not alone in this; ask any speaker how they feel before giving a speech. If they are being honest with you, they'll say they get nervous too, but have learned to control those nerves. It's all about rehearsal, practice, refining and doing, and doing it again.

In summary:

Eye contact is not only essential, but will help eliminate fear.

Feed on the DESIRE not the fear.

Self-talk yourself POSITIVE, "I can do this, Iwill do this."

Learn, rehearse, refine, do it. Learn, rehearse, refine, do it again.

Visualize yourself doing a great job in front of the audience.

Deal with mess-ups in a positive way.

And … breathe.

Chapter 11: Benefits Of Becoming An Ace Presenter And Why Giving A Great Presentation Matters

You probably already appreciate the importance of giving a great presentation – you've purchased a book on it, after all! However, to motivate you even further and reveal all the benefits of becoming a great presenter, I have listed some reasons why being able to give an excellent presentation is so damn useful:

It's a high-demand (and potentially well-paying) skillset to develop. The best public speaking professionals can command six-figure paychecks for their speeches. Now, you're not about to enter that league simply by reading this book; but by becoming better at giving presentations, you will ultimately join a high-value niche of individuals. And even though six figures per speech is a distant dream at present, it isn't unreasonable to think that becoming great at presenting will push your career forward. Think promotions, pay-raises, better jobs, and opportunities—all from putting the advice of this little book into action.

Becoming an excellent presenter is transferable to other important areas and skillsets. Sales is the best example. Becoming adroit at giving presentations is very similar to the techniques and principles used for sales situations like cold-calling, business pitches, one-on-one selling, etc. All involve presenting yourself and your ideas. Therefore, applying the advice of this book will develop skills that can apply to other roles (roles that are also high-value and potentially money-making). Sales, management, marketing, customer service – these all share many characteristics with presenting and will be improved by implementing the advice in this book. Does hitting two birds with one stone sound good? Hitting half a dozen is even better.

Giving presentations can become a vehicle for other goals. Imagine a work environment where someone in your team has to pitch a presentation about a new product the company is developing. If you believe in this product and see its future value, you might volunteer yourself to give that presentation – not so much because you love presentations (though what's not to love!?), but because you know it's a great route to becoming deeply familiar with a product you believe in. Preparing and giving a presentation is always a fantastic way to revise, memorize, and understand a topic.

Relax. Breathe. And Try to Take the Pressure Off

One of the reasons you are reading this book is – no doubt – because you fear the worst.

Imagine the scene: it's crunch time, and you're standing in front of your peers who are watching you with beady, expectant eyes. For whatever reason, it isn't happening as well as you'd like it to, and you know the presentation isn't going right. And now slight nerves are creeping in, which in turn twist in your stomach, and spread out into waves of panic throughout your body. You can't think clearly and can't remember what to say next. Sweat forms on your brow, and into your mind creep desperate hopes of a sudden emergency that forces everyone out of the room, offering an end to this torture.

I'm not going to lie; this happens. But this needn't happen to you, and don't worry—that is the last time we will run through that nightmare scenario.

However, there is an important lesson to glean from the above scenario:

Don't let emotions or stress overload you at any point.

Below are three great reasons why being aware of emotional stress and managing it are so important to giving a great presentation.

Stress and/or any negative emotional overwhelm can spiral quickly. From a small sense of things being too difficult, if you don't manage it, you can soon feel MUCH worse.

A calm, relaxed emotional state leads to a calm and relaxed delivery. This will mean that your audience will understand you better, and they will be more likely to get onboard with your ideas and to take the action you want them to take.

If you look nervous, people are less likely to take you and your presentation seriously.

So, how can you reel in the pressures, and feel relaxed and confident, no matter how important the presentation, or how inexperienced you are?

Breathe. This is a big one. Before you begin your presentation, take controlled, deep breaths – count 3 seconds in, then 3 seconds out. Doing this for just a few minutes will help your mind and mood "settle."

Throughout the presentation, make sure you take small pauses. This will help your ideas "land" with your audience, but it also gives you a moment to become conscious of your breathing again. Similarly, if you feel overwhelmed at any point, take this as a sign to pause and breathe.

If you have more time to spare before your presentation, and/or if you have experience of it, meditate briefly. Just sitting for 10 minutes in a comfortable position whilst focusing on your breath – 3 seconds in, 3 seconds out – will make a meaningful difference.

Manage lifestyle aspects, especially closer to the time of the presentation. Being well-slept, getting a bit of exercise in, and having a healthy breakfast all contribute to emotional stability and your ability to manage stress.

Though it is helpful to be relaxed and aware of your breathing, don't let this be to the detriment of a focused and upbeat energy in the presentation itself.

Find The Venue Beforehand and Turn it into Your Living Room

Visiting the venue before the time of the presentation is helpful. The main reason for this is obvious:

It will ensure that you give the presentation on time.

If you want to give the best presentation, a late arrival is simply unacceptable. Being late may mean that you have less time to prepare yourself and your resources, or even that you eat into your own presentation time. The worst-case scenario is that you don't find the venue at all and miss your own presentation! Don't take that chance; make sure you know exactly how to get to the venue, and how long it takes to get there.

It is also helpful to familiarize yourself with the room/hall/lecture theatre in which you will be giving the presentation. Doing so has a variety of benefits:

You can get to know the resources you will be using. For example, if you are connecting your laptop to a projector, you can ensure you know exactly how to work it. This will save stress and ensure that any "technical difficulties" aren't caused by you, and can be dealt with in a calm manner.

Other oddities of the venue can also be taken into account. Maybe the lights aren't all working, or the chairs are very uncomfortable – you don't know until you check the environment yourself.

If you are using handouts or any kind of audience participation activities, you can troubleshoot and prepare for any contingencies ahead of time.

You will generally feel more at ease and less worried when you do give the presentation. Indeed, the more familiar you are with the venue, the better the presentation you will give. Make it feel like your living room, and imagine everyone as guests in it. This will help you to give a more relaxed, focused talk, focused 100% on the delivery.

Consider taking this "make it feel like your living room" advice to the limit. No, don't put cushions down on the floor and bring your cat! But do spend time there in the hours or days previous to the talk. Ideally, you should practice giving your presentation there to really build your comfort.

When you practice at home, or even daydream about your presentation, you can visualize yourself in the exact environment. This will bring extra life to your visualizations and practice sessions, again resulting in improved focus and relaxation when you give the final talk.

Being aware of exits and entrances is also handy. You want to know where you will be entering and leaving the venue, as well as being aware of where latecomers to your talk might appear from.

The above is an exhaustive approach to familiarizing yourself with a venue. However, at a minimum:

Visit the venue beforehand to ensure that you won't be late on the day.

Spend one minute looking around, so there at least aren't any odd aspects that will surprise you, **e.g.**, a broken projector, not enough chairs, etc.

Chapter 12: Signs Of Public Speaking Fears And Anxieties

Glossophobia is a term that refers to the fear of public speaking. It comes from the Greek words **glössa** meaning tongue, and phobos meaning fear. Glossophobia is the term professionals use to denote a severe fear or anxiety of any form of public speaking. Individuals with this kind of fear may find themselves naturally averse to speaking in front of a group of people, or speaking at all in any kind of assembly. Below are the signs that point towards public speaking fears and anxieties. They are classified into physical, verbal, non-verbal signs.

Physical Signs of Glossophobia
Excessive sweating
Individuals who fear public speaking often begin sweating too much, before and during their speech performance. Some even sweat after they have finished speaking.

Sweating is a sure sign of nervousness and anxiety. Though some of the best speakers also experience bouts of sweating prior to their performance, they are able to control their nervousness, and effectively channel it into the volume, tone, and impact of their speech. People with **Glossophobia** are unable to do this. They sweat all throughout their speech, and are acutely aware of the way they look to their audience. This knowledge only makes them even more nervous, thus their bodies produce more sweat as a response to the environmental stress.

Uncontrollable shaking

This sign is usually seen together with excessive sweating. People who suffer from public speaking fears and anxieties are usually unable to control the shaking of their hands or in some cases, their whole bodies. This is especially obvious when the individual is holding cue cards before an assembly. The audience will be able to see the physical manifestation of his or her anxiety due to the speaker's uncontrollable shaking. In some instances, this shaking of the limbs or body is transferred to or affects the voice of the speaker. The speaker's voice then becomes ragged or stunted—yet another sign that the speaker is suffering from speaking anxiety or fear.

Hand wringing or excessive use of a single gesture

Hand wringing in a public speaker is a classic sign of Glossophobia. The repetitive use of a single gesture, such as nose touching or scratching, forehead massaging, or neck scratching, is the body's way of showing that it is uncomfortable or under a lot of stress. This is also usually seen with excessive sweating.

Other physical signs of Glossophobia include increased heart rate, pain in neck and back muscles before, during, and after a speech, nausea, panic attacks and difficulty breathing.

Verbal Signs of Glossophobia

Tense or High-pitched voice

Of course, there are people who naturally have a high-pitched or tense-sounding voice. However, individuals who suffer from **Glossophobia** are prone to sounding tense or high-pitched even if their voices are natural baritones or altos. Uncontrollable or unplanned changes in the tone and volume of a speaker's voice all point to nervousness and anxiety. Yes, good speakers can change the tone of their voice at will, but people with **Glossophobia** cannot. They are made to feel even more helpless or afraid when, in the middle of a speech, the tone of their voice changes without them meaning to.

Stuttering or stammering

While stuttering and stammering are two speech behaviors that can be easily corrected, people with Glossophobia often stutter or stammer repeatedly, even if they have no history of such speech behaviors. Their anxieties make them feel tongue-tied, or hinder their brains from focusing on what they are supposed to say, and in what order they must deliver their speech.

Non-verbal Signs of **Glossophobia**

Rapid blinking

A speaker who is rapidly blinking all throughout his or her speech is most likely suffering from a public speaking fear or anxiety. It is another response of the body to stress, and signals that the individual is operating under the fight or flight system.

Hand jerking or sudden, uncontrolled body movements

In response to a threatening or extremely stressful situation, the body releases adrenaline into its system to make the individual more alert and highly reactive. This is manifested through sudden and unexplainable hand jerking or other limb movements.

There are other signs that show if an individual has Glossophobia or other milder public speaking anxieties. All of them make the speaker dizzy or suddenly tired. They also drain the speaker's self-confidence and are often the sources of mistakes in an otherwise good performance. If you have many of the signs described in this chapter, then you must certainly read the next two chapters to learn what causes pubic speaking anxiety and how you can address these fears correctly and effectively.

Chapter 13: Public Speaking And Speech Anxiety

Unless you have chosen a career where public speaking is necessary, you will find that apart from classroom exercises, not everyone gets a chance to speak in public.

Public speaking is an activity, where you have a speaker delivering a message to an audience. This means that in order to speak in public, you have to be important enough to have an audience who will listen to you. This is why most public speeches come from leaders–people whose opinions and decisions are highly valued.

Think about it–those who are asked to give some kind of "public speech" have to be important in some way: a guest speaker for a conference has to be knowledgeable and well-experienced; a person who gives welcome remarks for a particular event usually hold a high position or play a key role in a certain company or community. At a wedding, you need to have an important role in the lives of the bride and groom in order to deliver a speech.

The reason you probably decided to further study public speaking is because you found yourself to be in a position of importance. If this is the case, be glad, and get ready to learn, as public speaking is essential to your success. Note that public speaking is an activity that has informed, persuaded, motivated, united, and inspired people for centuries.

Did You Know?

There was a time in the history of the ancient Greeks when they had no lawyers! A person charged with a crime had to defend himself by speaking to an audience, persuading them that he was not guilty.

Now before you proceed to reading this book, it is useful to have an understanding of the role of public speaking in your life– will you use it to build your career, support your interests, or influence people in general? In addition, set specific goals which you want to achieve. For example:

Deliver a 3-minute speech about myself (Week 1)

Deliver a 10-minute informative speech/lecture about my company/school (Week 2)

Deliver a 3-minute impromptu speech about a topic chosen by my friend

Every time public speaking is discussed, speech anxiety closely follows as a subtopic. This is not surprising since speaking in public is cited by most people as among their most dreadful fears, ranking closely to people's fear of death!

So what explains this seemingly irrational fear of public speaking? It has something to do with people's fear of losing credibility, and being in a position of vulnerability, possible failure, and criticism. Note that you get a feeling of anxiety not only at times when you are about to deliver a public speech; it happens whenever you are going to do something important, or something which can affect your ability to succeed.

Did You Know?

The symptoms of speech anxiety include having a dry mouth, cold/sweaty hands, and a quivering voice. Anxiety can also take the form of nervous shaking, excessive use of fillers (uh's and um's), avoiding eye contact, stiff posture and increased perspiration. In some cases, people who experience speech anxiety also have acute hearing.

Now that you understand what speech anxiety is, along with its symptoms, remember that experiencing speech anxiety is actually quite normal. Even seasoned public speakers get to experience a little nervousness when they deliver a speech! However, audiences hardly ever notice because these speakers know how to control and manage the anxiety they experience. This is also what you need to learn.

Completely putting your speech anxiety under control will take some time; yes it will take practice. You will need to deliver several speeches and build your confidence over time. However, here are three very specific ways to help control your stage fright:

Prepare sufficiently for your speech. This means you need to be physically, mentally, and emotionally prepared for it. Have enough sleep, eat well, and drink enough water so you won't get dehydrated. Know your speech by heart–you should be able to talk about your topic first thing in the morning and last thing before you go to bed. Finally, be excited enough about your speech. Fall in love with it! You should be able to deliver it with enthusiasm.

Find friendly faces in the audience. This will help make you feel at ease, but in the absence of friendly faces, just smile, make eye contact, and begin your speech.

Move. Use appropriate actions/hand gestures. Anxiety can either make you look stiff and still, or jittery and unsteady. Expect yourself to have some kind of excess energy and use this to make your speech more exciting. Channel that excess energy to the use of appropriate hand gestures and actions that can help emphasize your words.

Taking deep breaths and calming your mind will certainly help you manage your speech anxiety. When you begin delivering your speech, you will find that it becomes easier as you go along. In case you forget a part of your speech or experience a mental block, just relax and think about the message that you want to deliver. Slowly, but surely, endeavor to get yourself back to the topic and back to your audience.

You can consider public speaking as a larger version of the usual conversation. Its setting is more formal and you may have more participants (audiences), but consider all of them as normal people, who just came to listen to what you have to say.

Like life's battles, your battle with speech anxiety is first won in the mind. You need to conquer it! Think of the worst thing that could ever happen–perhaps you'd stutter, forget your speech or worse, throw up. People will talk about you for a while, and if you're a bit popular, you might be bullied via the social media. But what happens after that? It ends. People will forget, and someone else will do something new. See? Even the worst experiences will come to pass!

Of course, you're not reading this book for nothing. You're reading it because public speaking will give you your most fulfilling experiences in life. It will shape your career. It will bring you to different places. It will enable you to reach out to a variety of individuals. It will make you more confident. It will be a part of who you are. You will be an excellent public speaker.

Chapter 14: Audience Participation

The connection between speaker and audience is always two-way. However, it is you, the speaker, who must be the one to get the ball rolling.

Involving your audience in the process in some small way can help to relax you and make you feel less isolated, and can also do the same for them.

You could ask for a show of hands to see where the audience are from. I did this once when doing a poetry reading and it turned out I was the only person in the room who did not go to the local university. I pointed this out, made a joke of it and even received a good-natured round of applause. In doing this, I got to know my audience a little better.

If you are doing a humorous speech or stand-up comedy set about your experiences of working in retail or catering, you could ask for a show of hands to see who has also worked in this field in the past.

You could ask the audience a series of questions and let them raise their hands and try to tell you the answers.

Alternatively, you could flip this on its head, and allocate a section of your speaking slot to answering questions from the audience.

Question-and-answer sessions are important, as they can give the audience a chance to clarify something the speaker has already said, or to raise an issue which they feel is important that has not yet been addressed. Through this, the speaker can show the audience that their views and opinions are valued, and that listening to them and trying to understand their point-of-view is a priority.

Similarly, giving the audience a chance to vote on something related to the talk or evening as a whole can be very effective (and can sometimes be made fun).

The speaker could even invite members of the audience up to the stage (or equivalent area) to help them to demonstrate something.

For example, if you were giving a talk about how to improve interview technique, you could invite a member of the audience to come up to the stage to act out a job interview role-play with you. This could make the audience feel more involved in the process, and show them a practical example of how certain interview techniques could be used. The audience may also find the role-play entertaining if it is done well.

Some of the best live music shows I have seen (and I have seen a lot over the years) have involved the band or singer-songwriter inviting particular sections of the crowd to join in with singing the song in question after demonstrating what they need to do and when. Done well, this can greatly increase the sense of unity, not just between members of the audience who did not know each other previously, but also between the audience and the performer.

Actors in pantomimes frequently encourage audiences to repeat silly and over-the-top sounds or words at appropriate moments throughout performances. This is a big part of the reason why this type of performance is so popular, especially among families with young children.

Motivational speakers often attempt to rally their audiences by encouraging them to repeat an empowering message after them as an affirmation or incantation. They could also achieve a similar effect by encouraging the audience to repeat an empowering physical action with them. This can be a great way of involving them and giving them something memorable they can take away and use after the talk has finished.

If the audience feel they have gained something from the experience that will carry over into their day-to-day lives in a positive way, hopefully the talk will have done what it set out to do, and the speaker will have won over their audience.

Chapter 15: So You Don't Like Your Audience?

As its name suggest, public speaking wouldn't be complete without an audience or public listening to it. Who would appreciate and clap for your speech if you'll deliver it in front of empty chairs right? Though starring at empty seats is a tad more comforting than seeing actual people, it removes the real essence and challenge of public speaking. And doing so somehow degrades the art.

Your audience are the ones who share the experience of your talking engagement with you. They participate to benefit from the two-way relationship that you've built the moment you stepped on stage. Observing, hand raising and answering your questions are some of the ways to show participation and interaction during a speech. Also, modest clapping, giving of questions and comments as well as airing feedback after a presentation may also be expected from them.

Audiences vary in different ways. More often than not, the type and purpose of the event determine the important characteristics of an audience. These determine the needs you ought to satisfy as a speaker when you decide to deliver an audience-centered talk.

Age is one of the most common factors to be considered in public speaking. Knowing whether you are performing in front of kids, teenagers or adults may help you decide on what topic to focus on. Moreover, knowing this will help you determine the appropriateness of the language you will use among other considerations. Having a picture of the socio-economic background of the audience is also important. Their cultural diversity and economic status are key factors when it comes to building an understanding of and relating to your speech. You can not expect a group of A-class people to relate to a speech about the difficulties of taking public transportation during rush hour right? And lastly, listening styles of the audience should be considered to ensure that you obtain and sustain their attention.

But of course, who has not heard of the horror stories on audiences from down under right? These groups of people may be cold, unresponsive and offensive for many reasons. It may be a result of bad timing, unfavourable speaking skills or other external factors that brings their attention away from what you are saying. Others can get really nasty where in they sleep or talk as you in a hostile manner. As a speaker, you are expected to respect and treat your audience right at all times despite their unbecoming behaviour. It is very much part of the challenges that public speaking offers. So what should you do in these circumstances you ask? Below are a couple of things that you can practice to keep your cool in front your audience to beat all odds.

• Gain rapport once you step on stage – exude confidence to command attention for them to stop and notice you.

• It is best to try some ice breakers or just jokes at the beginning of your speech to make them comfortable with your presence.

• Be open to changes throughout your speech to suit the needs or desires of your audience. Public speaking is a dynamic process from the moment you begin preparations.

• Don't get them bored! Unless you are a movie star or famous celebrity, your audience wouldn't like to hear a self-centered speech from you. Of course mentioning about your experiences and achievements from time to time is acceptable but please don't make everything about you. Place the needs of your audience at the forefront to gain their favour.

It is not a good idea to react in anger or frustration when things aren't going right. Just keep calm and continue on your speech because you have a number of people in your audience – chances are others who are also sitting in front of you appreciate your speech.

Favourite Beginner Topics

Being the new kid is never easy. More often than not, you get pushed around, trampled and picked on when you're still not familiar with how things work. You just can't seem to get a good piece of the pie when you're a new. That is if you get any at all.

This circumstance doesn't only happen when you're new in school or the work place. This may also happen when you're a beginner at doing something like cheerleading, playing the piano or creative writing. A sad fact but true – experts may at some times eat you alive. Though not all of them have a vested interest in your skill or the lack of it, consider yourself lucky if you find an honest to goodness mentor that is willing to train and hone your skills. But don't bet on it.

At one point or another in our lives, we become a newbie at something. A perfect example of this is our own personal journey in life. Being born in this chaotic world doesn't come with an instruction manual so figuring things is left entirely up you. Of course, we have our family and friends who are going though their own journeys as well. And chances are they've encountered the same or anything similar to the circumstances that we're facing making them credible sources. Though each one of us technically goes thorough life on our own, we all have an overflowing reservoir of guides and resources that can help us through.

So what does that have to do with public speaking right? Well as a newbie in the terrifying field of public speaking, I would just like to share with you a wonderful principle that you can hold on to not only in public speaking but in your other endeavours as well. **Being a newcomer should never hinder you to excel in anything that you desire to do.** Everything is specifically difficult when you're starting up so just hold on.

To lighten up your load a little bit, here are some topics that new public speakers can explore. Pick the topic that you have the most knowledge on. Doing so will help feel more comfortable as you inform or persuade your public.

- Abortion
- Alcohol and substance abuse
- AIDS/HIV
- Addiction
- Dieting
- Euthanasia
- Genetically modified organisms
- Global warming
- Natural calamities
- Endangered species

- Agricultural policies
- Littering & vandalism
- Biodiversity
- Free trade
- Security situations in other countries
- Travel bans
- Natural wonders of the world
- Race relations
- Gender equality
- Teen pregnancy
- Marriage & divorce
- Organ donation
- Terrorism
- Crimes on the internet
- Government elections
- Financial management
- Violence (in school, at home or among teens)
- Tax reforms
- Child labour
- Sensorship
- Piracy

The topics listed above are merely suggestions based on common use and availability of resources for research. You may choose any topic that suit your skills and purpose as well. For a broader choice, you may look at current events or issues under health, business, travel, social issues and politics to name a few. Be sure to consider the timeliness as well the use of the topic of your choice.

Chapter 16: Know Your Audience

Most of the time, the audience wants to be entertained or enlightened. They want you to succeed.

Sometimes your fear is not rational. You have to teach it to be rational. You can teach fear to be rational by proving to it in a logical manner that everything is okay.

This is what we will do here.

In the intro of this book, I mentioned that as a child I was terrified of giving my speech in church. As I look back now, I realize that the people there wanted to see me succeed at doing my little poem.

They wanted to hear the little cute words that I would say.

If you are giving a sales meeting, the salespeople there want to know how to improve their sales. They want you to succeed at giving them information so that they can make more sales.

Now, I won't ignore the fact that there are situations that things could go badly. So what do you do?

Make sure you are thoroughly prepared. What I mean by that is to make sure that your message and/or your performance is ready.

Here's how…

1) Do your presentation in front of a mirror.

2) Record yourself doing the presentation.

3) Do your presentation one on one with someone you feel most comfortable with at first.

Remember to be standing so that you can start practicing your body language.

1)Next, do your presentation in front of 3 people.

2) Do your presentation in front of a small group (5-15 people)

You may start to feel a little anxious as you move up, but this will help you to build up your resistance to talking to bigger audiences.

Finally, get out there and deliver your message, because you will never feel 100% ready to do it. Just do it. PERIOD. NO excuses.

Give your body a chance to get used to the exposure and start learning to deal with giving your message to multiple people at once.

Trust that your body will adjust to the exposure.

Chapter 17: Look And Feel Confident

Fake it 'til You Make It, that's what most people say. And you know what? It is actually true.

I have a little story to share. You know Bruce Springsteen, don't you? He's one of the most popular musicians of all time, and is also known to suffer from nerves— especially before performing. But, do his nerves stop him from performing and doing what he likes best? Of course not.

See, you can actually be nervous without it showing. In short, you have to fake your confidence and eventually, you'll notice you're actually not faking anything anymore, and you're really confident already!

Dress for the Occasion

One good way of feeling confident onstage is by looking the part.

You see, people tend to listen to those who look as if they really know what they are talking about, as opposed to those who look like they just passed by the event for nothing. You don't have to buy extremely expensive clothes, but it would help if you could invest on a few important pieces (slacks, a formal dress, some ties, leather shoes, etc) so that once you get asked to talk in front of an audience, you'd get to show them that you are ready.

Try it. Dress up for a certain event that you're invited to and you'd feel like you actually belongs there, instead of just feeling like you're just there to pass time. If you want to belong, dress and act like it—and you will.

Focus on those who nod their heads

When speaking in front of a crowd, you'd be able to notice who are listening by checking out who are nodding their heads, and who are actually making sense of what you're talking about. Now, focus on those people so you'd also get responses and so the rest of the audience will feel compelled to butt—or blend—in, and listen to you more intently.

Be mindful of gestures and body language

Another way to make sure that you look and feel confident is by being mindful of body language. Here are some tips that you can keep in mind:

Make use of space. You can move around the stage. You don't have to dance, but you can walk from one end to the next in order to engage your audience. It would be so awkward if you'd just stay in place all the time, looking like a stiff tree. You can walk. You can help them understand your thoughts better by making your way to them, or at least, helping them see you as a person and not a talking stick.

Stop shifting focus. When you look from one side of the audience to the other in such a quick manner, people will feel like you're rolling your eyes or that you are extremely nervous. Yes, it's okay to make use of space—but do not try to look from one person to another as if asking for approval. That's not the kind of message you'd want to impart on your audience.

Be animated! As Tyra Banks would say, **Smile**! Smile with your eyes. When you do this, it shows that you're sincere with what you're doing instead of just looking bored and stiff and not knowing what to say. It makes you more alive and realistic—and that's the kind of speaker people want.

Make use of open gestures. Point your hands outwards, don't just point to your chest and think that people could understand what you're trying to say.

Don't make it verbatim. You don't have to prepare and type a long speech and read every single word the way it was written. This would be so monotonous and would just make your audience bored. You can adlib—this is your speech, after all! The more natural it is the better!

Think about the gestures you use every day, especially when you're at the dinner table, or when talking to people closest to you—and use them for your speech. This way, you'd be way more natural!

Avoid these mannerisms:

Touching your face.

Playing with your fingers.

Shifting your weight or swaying from side to side.

Playing with your pens.

Putting hands in your pockets.

Touching your ears.

Adjusting your hair.

Pacing back and forth.

Crossing the arms.

Arranging clothes over and over again.

Make them laugh

Laughter is not only the best medicine, it's also one of the easiest ways to get someone's attention and to keep atmosphere light and engaging. It's not about making slapstick jokes, but just about showing your wit and being able to make the conversation fun for everyone.

Just because you're making a speech doesn't mean it has to be overly serious, especially when you know that you can inject some humor in it. When laughter ensues in a room, people feel better and they feel like they could reach you, instead of feeling like you're only talking about the things that matter to you. But of course, don't try to make jokes if it's a serious matter (i.e., death, grieving, etc.) Think of your audience.

Your speech should be about everyone—and not just about you!

Don't mind your mistakes

Another cliché: Everyone makes mistakes. No one is perfect and no one is immune to errors and the like—but will you actually let those mistakes get you down? No, of course not.

What you should do is just get back up. If you said a wrong word, don't make use of fillers (more on this in the next chapter); Try a few seconds of silence, and then make a joke, or just engage the audience.

When you recognize your mistakes, you'd easily be able to bounce back from them instead of just feeling like you are a failure. Even the most seasoned public speakers make mistakes. Don't let those errors make you fall off track!

Chapter 18: Understanding Word Power

"A man is filled with what comes from his mouth and is nourished by what his lips provide. The tongue has power over life and death, those who like speaking will eat its fruit" (The Bible 18:20- 21)

The ancient Hindu Vedas says that the very beginning of the universe was with words, it says, "In the beginning was Brahman with whom was the Word, and the Word is Brahman." We get similar lines in holy Bible John wrote, "In the beginning was the Word, and the Word was with God, and the Word was God." It is also said that "The Word is God" (John 1:1). It is interesting to note that the word 'Universe' is a combination of two words: Uni, meaning 'one' and Verse, meaning 'word' or 'body of words'. Hence, 'Universe' is 'collection of word'.

In India, it is believed that, the world is a reflection of infinite combinations of sound vibration. The Sanskrit alphabet starts from "a" and ends with "ksha". The alphabet is called "akshara", which literally means "infallible" or "supreme". In Ancient India, the "aksharas" (letters) are considered as "bijas", or seeds of existence. The sacred Hindu Scripture Veda is full of the importance of the power of sound.

Words changed water crystals

Dr. Masaru Emoto, in his wellresearched book, "The Miracle of Water", gives thoughtful insights on the power of words on water. He demonstrated that when water is exposed to good words, good crystals result. He further mentioned that words are vibrations, and when our bodies, comprising of 70 percent water, are exposed to good words, we experience health and well-being. On the same line, negative words create bad vibrations. Hence, the choice of words creates the corresponding life. Masaru Emoto demonstrated that the most beautiful crystals are those formed after the water is exposed to the words love and gratitude.

Words, words and words

The advanced practitioners of Shamanism and hypnotism could influence a person to either feel good or bad about himself with words. They could open up the deep recesses of their subconscious mind. The life coach like Anthony Robbins has cured decade-old stammerer, prevented many people from committing suicide and reconciled the fighting couples from divorce by his power of words. In India, we have thousands of stories and tales narrating incidents where, angered Sadhu's curse turns a person into stone or plant or lifelong affliction. Similarly, when pleased such Sadhu's blessing brings prosperity and success to people and even frees them from the curse. Their words used to carry so much power. Hence, words are powerful in themselves and it becomes more powerful corresponding to the personality of the person uttering it.

Neuro-Linguistic programme (NLP)

Further, when I came across few amazing books on NLP and attended the live seminars of life coaching, I was convinced, that the use of right words can do wonders. Just reframing the questions and self-inner conversation to oneself bring about a total change in the way we look at particular things, person and feel about ourselves and others. He who knows how to use the words or reframe the question or conversation can do wonders.

The right words when used with intensity are powerful to create electric impulse, affecting us on the physical, emotional and spiritual level.

As a test read out the words on the left and the right columns:

Negative   expression   Problem
Confused
Lost
Empowering   expression   Challenge
Curious
Searching

Unemployed		lonely
Insulted		
Failure		
Ignored		
Thin		
Taking	break	Available
Misunderstood		Feedback
Focused		
Slim		

Does it not create different feeling and mindset? Indeed, it does. The business world, sociologists and HR managers have intelligently found better words over a period of time. Here are the few more examples:

Old	nomenclature	Housewife
Fat		
Disabled	child	Peon
Used		car
Driver		
Expulsion	letter	Bribe
Prisoners		
Servant		
New		nomenclature

Homemaker

Horizontally challenged/plus size

Differently abled/ Special child Attendant

Pre-owned car

Chauffeur

Pink Slip

Speed money

Inmates

Domestic help

You must have realized that how change of words gives totally different mindset, experience and feeling. If you observe closely all the power is derived through the ability to communicate and the ability to persuade. If you have no money, you can persuade someone to lend you some money, for instance, Dhirubhai Ambani started with little amount of money but persuaded the investors to invest and went on to build one of the biggest company in India. Similarly, all the start-up ventures progress when the founder is able to communicate and persuade the venture capitalist about their idea or product. If you want to end injustice like colonialism, racism, you have to persuade people to fight for it as demonstrated by Gandhiji, Martin Luther and Nelson Mandela. Even winning a beautiful woman, is less about your physical appearance and more about how you can communicate. Anything in life can be achieved with the power of communication. Persuasive and effective communication are one of the most important life skills you can develop.

Self-effort is like carrying a bucket and whereas with powerful communication skill, you create a pipeline where thousands of other people support you with their talent, time, money etc. towards your cause or goal. Hence, communication is the power tool, it's a multiplier. It creates leverage. However, it is important to remember that plain, unemotional words do not create influence. One needs to intensely feel what one is conveying, as it is the confidence, faith and persona behind the words that begets the real power.

Each word carries a vibration which is multiplied by the presence of the speaker. The human history is shaped by our great leaders and thinkers who have used the power of words to lift us out of slumber and create a difference by implanting the ideas that have transformed millions. They have inspired us to join in their causes and thereby shaped the course of history for good.

Words shape life

Who you are today is the result of what words you have listened to since your childhood. Our beliefs are formed by words and they can be changed by words as well. If you are born to a rich family, you would be tuned towards abundance, luxury and higher goals whereas if you are born in a poor family, you will be attuned towards necessities of life i.e, a job, house and savings for rainy days. Even at nation's level, it is the power of words that shapes their attitude and approach. USA, Germany, Israel etc. represent the philosophy of power and domination whereas, countries like Bhutan, Japan, India are towards harmonious living.

We can use on our own the power of words to live a better life at emotional, social, personal and spiritual level. We can overcome problems, by calling them challenges, failures, by calling them feedback, physical ailment, by calling them the timely signal for opting healthy lifestyle etc. The moment you change your vocabulary, your entire approach and attitude get transformed. Rich words make your life richer. Good vocabulary empowers. Hence, wise people choose their words very carefully as they realize the words create an experience. "The words that we attach to our experience become our experience." (Anthony Robbins).

You can distinguish between people with their words. A person who is optimist and gregarious would use the words like Wow, amazing, excellent, challenging, possible, we can, let's try etc. whereas the vocabulary of pessimist and negative person would include disgusting, hell, impossible, sickening, horrible, it's killing, I'm fed up, overwhelmed, hopeless, frustrated etc. Words shape our beliefs and affect our actions.

The power of words are immense, it can be used either positively or negatively. It can inspire people to sacrifice their life or take the life of innocent people. The power of words inspired freedom fighters to give up their life and it also inspires soldiers to give up their life for the nation.

The extremist uses the same power of words to brainwash youth to turn them into a terrorist or a jihadi. For instance, the American, John Walker Lindh, while studying Islamism went to various Islamic countries and even attended a lecture by Osama Bin Laden. Subsequently, he became a jihadi and fought against

American Army in Afghanistan in 2001. Such is the power of the word.

Research has shown that the 'Maha Mrityunjaya mantra' improves health and increases happiness and peace of mind. It awakens a healing force and removes obstacles. Here's an example, if people around you keep on saying that you are a bad person, after some time, it will settle in your subconscious mind, and soon you will start believing and behaving in the same manner, popularly called the Pygmalion effect or Rosenthal effect. Therefore, by using words wisely, you can create a desired reality and make people support that reality."Words are, of course, the most powerful drug used by mankind." (Rudyard Kipling)

The voice carries ideas, convey information, shapes opinions, influence feelings, transform attitudes and make us act. A powerful speaker can inspire and vitalize or it can depress or sadden. He can make people act, react or remain calm at will. Your words can make your child a coward or brave, reserved or spontaneous, dependent or independent, depending on your daily communication with him.

Our life is shaped by the words we hear from our parents, teachers, colleagues, bosses, spouse, children and what we talk to ourselves. Often some situations in our life take paradigm shift due to some words. It could be encouraging words from your mentor, senior, spouse, children or it could even be the insult from people around. For instance, Kalidas, the renowned Indian writer, life got changed when his wife insulted him by saying that he is an ignorant person. Consequently, he became a scholar and wrote rich literature. Angulimal, the dreaded dacoit got transformed with few words of Gautam Buddha.

There is no end to the examples and anecdotes to substantiate the immense power of words. Look closely and you will observe that words truly shapes our life.

Chapter 19: Learning From Famous Public Speakers

The greatest and most famous public speakers of time started just like you. Once, in their childhood, they were also nervous and afraid, even more than what you are feeling right now. These people started out small, but because of their willingness, effort, commitment, and passion, they were able to improve into an effective public speaker. How did they become the person that they are today? How did they overcome their fear in public speaking? What do they have to tell aspiring public speakers like you? This chapter will share to you some insights about the world's greatest public speakers to help you improve your public speaking skills.

Warren Buffet was a billionaire who once feared public speaking, but has managed to overcome it over time. According to Buffet, fear is necessary. He even doubted that the greatest public speakers of time would become successful if they did not encounter fear and nervousness. The goal, according to Buffet, is not to try to eliminate fear, but to be able to manage it properly. Fear and nervousness in delivering public speech are actually normal and helpful if managed properly.

Another great public speaker is Winston Churchill. He was the prime minister of United Kingdom from 1940 to 1945. According to Churchill, whenever you need to speak in public, you should get straight to the point and "hit the mark". Once you are decided about the topic that you wish to target, focus on it and go back to it every time. Make sure that you direct the points that you are making towards your topic so that you will not be diverting to different topics. This will only cause your speech to become ambiguous and unclear. He also compared a good speech to a woman's skirt. He said that the length of the speech should be moderate; neither too long nor too short, so that it will be able to cover the topic thoroughly and create interest.

Finally, Dale Carnegie was a lecturer on speech development, especially on public speaking and salesmanship. He is an expert when it comes to improving public speaking skills. Like any other public speakers, he began just like any one of us who are afraid, even terrified, to speak in public. He reminds aspiring public speakers like you to consider emotion whenever you are engaged in a public speaking activity. Carnegie teaches us to that the people we are dealing with whenever we speak in public are creatures of emotions. Thus, not only do we have to impart information to them, we also have to appeal to their emotions. In that way the audience will remember us, and what we said. In conquering your public speaking fear, Carnegie suggests that you do something about it, and not just sit around and think about your speech all day. You should practice at all times until you finally deliver it perfectly. He also emphasizes on the importance of mind conditioning in conquering fears. Always be positive that you can do it.

Mentioned above are just some of the remarkable people who have contributed to the enhancement of our public speaking skills. They have gone a long way in public speaking even if they started out as nervous and as afraid as you. Through these famous public speakers, you now know how to overcome fear, and that it is possible to overcome it. Fear is necessary and you do not have to get rid of it. You only need to manage it properly.

Through the help of the insights of these people, you can be inspired to be just like them one day. You only need courage and passion. Who knows you will be the next greatest public speaker of your time?

Chapter 20: What Is Public Speaking

What is Public Speaking?

Public speaking is the process of making your views and ideas public by speaking to a group of people in a structured manner.

Almost all people will say that giving public speaking is difficult because it involves some preparations, practices and certainly combating anxieties. Bear in mind that stage fright of speaking in public is the most commonly experienced fear. Therefore, you should not change your course, find other careers or quit to join a club if speaking publicly is required on those fields. This implies that the most important guide to public speaking is by learning to accept the anxieties in that fear or fright of public speaking is normal. Experts of Psychology also some anxiety is good because it can increase one's ability.

On the other hand, technically, a guide to public speaking also usually emphasize on the introduction, body and conclusion.

Although the details of those there aspects can be various, those are basic of organizing ideas. You might want to write the body and it is followed by the introduction and conclusion because it has been proven more helpful. Further, introduction is used to get the audience' attention to focus on your speaking. Here, you should be very careful to address their needs, not yours. On the other hand, the conclusion is the part where you will stress and restate your ideas. Therefore, you should use some attention grabber such as jokes, anecdotes or quotation to end your speaking.

In order to improve your skill in delivering speeches, you should take every opportunity you can to speak. Facing various audiences regularly and speaking on various topics will reduce your anxiety whenever you have to speak before an audience. However, although speaking in a large may then become your habit, you should also know when to stop talking.

Incorporating these aspects will help you build credibility as a public speaker. Finally, once you become a credible public speaker you may make your own guide to public speaking.

Public speaking skills are essential to anyone aspiring to become a good communicator. Contrary to popular perception, public speaking skills are required not just by people who want to speak in public but by anyone who wants to get along well in life. This topic is not given the importance it deserves by many people who may think that speaking is something we do naturally and often and that it doesn't require any special skills. It is true that speaking is one activity you are engaged in for a longer time than in any other activity. It is all the more important that you are well equipped with something you do for a major part of our time. To succeed in any profession or calling, the most important skill required is the communication skill.

What are public speaking skills? One can list a number of components of this skill but I will classify them into two main categories - preparation and presentation.

Preparation is the most important requisite to be a successful communicator. If you are aspiring to be a public speaker, first concentrate on preparation. You may be surprised to learn that most of the good speakers spend a lot of time in preparing their speeches. Preparation involves understanding the context and scope. Who are the audience? What is the topic? What is the time you are expected to speak for? Depending on answers to this question, you can decide what is going to be the scope for your speech and at what level you have to handle the topic to suit the composition of the audience and the time limit.

Once you draw the contours of your speech, then think what the content should be, the sources from which you can collect information and how much of the information you can pack in your speech. These factors will define the outline of your speech. Once the outline is ready, then you can prepare the full text of the speech, building it upon the points you have decided to cover.

The second skill, the skill of presentation is definitely more important than the skill of preparation. There are thousands of speech writers working from behind but there are only a few to deliver speeches. You have to perfect your posture, tone, modulation and gestures, not to speak of several other subtle aspects like eye contact, face expression etc. Working on the delivery comes with hard work, practice and experience. You can start with observing how good speakers present their speeches.

SEVEN WAYS ON HOW TO OVERCOME YOUR FEAR OF PUBLIC SPEAKING

Have you ever avoided a career or business opportunity because it required you to speak publicly? Did you ever have a great idea you wanted to share in a group setting but didn't because of your fear of speaking in front of a group of people?

You are not alone in the fear of public speaking. In my travels, I have seen where the fear of public speaking have kept otherwise very successful people in all walks of life from achieving their full potential. When you let this fear dominate your life, you lose out on promotions, business opportunities, community activities, and most of all self-confidence.

The following are seven powerful ways of overcoming your fear of public speaking and achieving a new level of success in your career, your business, and your life:

Ask Yourself the Important Question

Ask yourself, "Where does my fear come from and is it real?" Was there a public speaking opportunity in the past that you think didn't go well or that you felt was poorly prepared? Maybe you had to stand up in front of your classmates in high school or college and someone made what you perceived as a negative comment concerning your presentation. Maybe you gave a good speech but you started to over analyze every detail of the speech.

First, realize that whatever happened did so at another time and place and you are no longer that person. With new experiences, you have grown into a more confident person with much to offer. Second, embrace feedback, extract the true areas of improvement from the feedback and work to improve your public speaking ability. Be honest and fair with yourself and determine if the feedback is coming from someone who is qualified to give quality feedback. I had one presentation skills student whose manager told her she was a poor speaker because she moved her hands and arms during the presentation. Was the manager giving qualified feedback? Doubtful. Yet, this manager's feedback affected this employee in a negative way for years until the employee became my coaching student.

Again, separate qualified feedback from unqualified feedback and learn from it. Also, don't allow negative public speaking situations that happen in the past apply to your present or future public speaking opportunities.

Face Your Fear of Public Speaking

The fastest way to overcome any fear, much less the fear of public speaking, is to face your fear and attack it. Look for and embrace opportunities to make presentations. Start with non threatening opportunities such as your children's school meeting or a non work related situation and work your way up to more important, high pressure situations such as work meetings.

Realize that each time you speak is an opportunity to improve your speaking ability. Look at your public speaking skills as a muscle. The more you exercise your public speaking muscle, the stronger it becomes and you will improve your speaking abilities.

Go into each public speaking opportunity with a clear set of goals. Maybe for your first speech, you may have a goal of eliminating "hums" and "ahs." For another speech you may have a goal of completing your speech with a powerful ending.

Visualize Your Public Speaking Success

Invest time the night before you speak to visualize what a successful speech looks, sounds, and feels like and how you will feel while giving it. If you don't see it yourself, it won't happen. Most presentations can be dramatically improved just by investing time ahead of the presentation to visualize a successful outcome.

Master the Material

Invest the time to know what you are presenting. Invest time to rehearse several variations of your speech.

Rehearse your speech as if something goes wrong. What if your PowerPoint goes down, you forget a section in your speech, or someone heckles you? How will you react? If you know your material well enough, you will be able to overcome any presentation challenge.

Master Your Public Speaking Mind

During a group coaching session, a presenter started speaking, made a mistake and promptly announced, "I hate speaking in public!" In this instance, she did not manage her public speaking mind, and let her fear of public speaking take over her performance.

When you make negative statements concerning public speaking, it will reinforce your fear of public speaking. Take the time to replace negative statements with positive public speaking affirmations.

Take Time to Analyze Your Performance

In most cases, we are our own toughest critics when speaking. Whenever you speak, videotape or audiotape your presentations, sit down, and honestly analyze your performance. Once you start to record your presentations, you will realize that some of the issues you were worried about aren't in your speech and you will instantly see areas of improvement and address them accordingly. As the old saying goes, "The video doesn't lie."

Ask for feedback from people you respect and who can give you quality, supportive feedback that will empower you to want apply the feedback in your next speech. Before your speech, tell the person you ask to give you feedback what your public speaking goals are and what you are working to improve.

Once you analyze your areas of improvement, immediately go out and exercise your public speaking muscle and apply the improvement.

Reward Yourself

Reward yourself for any improvements in your public speaking skills. The reward is up to you, but make sure to immediately reward yourself.

Bonus Public Speaking Secret: If you forget a word or a phrase during your speech, never apologize and keep speaking as though nothing happened. Unless the audience has a detailed transcript of your speech, they won't know what you forgot. Don't let the fear of forgetting something in your speech keep you from giving great speeches.

Now, go out and exercise your public speaking muscle to give outstanding presentations. When you apply the seven secrets to overcoming your fear of public speaking, you will realize more opportunities and gain a new level of confidence.

Chapter 21: Professional Public Speakers

Professional public speakers are usually hired to deliver public speeches in areas such as business, sporting or commercial events. Excellent public speaking skills are essential for those speaking in a professional capacity. Professional Public Speakers include among them ex-politicians, media personalities, sport stars and other public figures. They are usually hired for their expertise in a certain field. Their objective in delivering a speech can be wide ranging. They may wish to transmit information or inspire and motivate an audience. However, their speech may be simply to entertain an audience.

A professional public speaker either works independently or may be represented by a Speakers' Bureau. A Speakers' Bureau is a company that provides professional speakers for business or social events. A Speakers' Bureau acts as the speaker's agent and is paid on a commission basis. The commission is usually 25-30%. The speakers' bureau will facilitate the initial introduction between speaker and client. There are a few types of Speakers' Bureau. The first type are set up as commercial enterprises and will hold a data base of speakers, such as motivational speakers or keynote speaker or after-dinner speakers. This type of bureau provides professional speakers to their paying clients. The second type of Speakers' Bureau is situated within a business. The professional speaker is employed by the business to communicate company strategy. Many professional speakers also use a crowd-sourced model online, which connects speakers with potential clients in the online community.

Professional public speakers do have to work at refining their public speaking skills. They often undertake on-going training and education in order to improve their public speaking skills. Learning better story-telling techniques, learning how to use humour more effectively as a communication tool, keeping abreast of changes and doing research in their subject-matter, are some of the ways in which professional public speakers manage to stay at the top of their profession.

Rudolph Giuliani - former Mayor of New York

Professional public speakers are usually paid a speaking fee but it is not uncommon for high profile personalities to be paid exceptional sums for speaking engagements. For instance, in 2006, it was reported that Rudolph Giuliani, former mayor of New York, earned $11 Million in speaking fees and book income.

So, as you can see, it is possible for successful public speakers to earn vast amounts of money.

The Steps Outlined In Preparing And Delivering A Speech

Listed below is a summary that may be useful when preparing and delivering your speech.

☐ Research your topic;

☐ Prepare your speech – but do no over-prepare;
☐ Condense the information into bullet points – to highlight key points you wish to focus on;
☐ Practice your speech – do as many practice sessions as you feel are necessary;
☐ Practice calming exercises to help you to relax and to focus your mind;
☐ Be sure to project a confident and self-assured attitude when you walk onto the stage or stand up to deliver your speech. Body language is an important indicator as to how a person is feeling and your audience will be able to tell whether you are feeling confident or not;
☐ Speak directly to your audience;
☐ Do no rush your speech : speak at an even pace so that you can control your delivery;
☐ If you begin to feel anxious or stressed during your speech, pause for a few seconds, and take deep, slow gentle

breaths, to help you relax and regain focus;
☐Always maintain a positive attitude.

Chapter 22: The Same Conference But Different People

Just as our faces, complexion and personalities are different, so are our human wants and needs are different and infinite.

The Eternal Secret to Business Success

Even if you have two identical twins with the same 46 chromosomes from the same household, trained and nurtured by the same parents, attended the same institution and grew up in the same environment, still their wants and needs would differs from each other!

That is the reason why if one is inspired by a particular word, phrase or music, the other would remain totally unmovable, uninterested and could be bored by the same word, phrase and music.

So the jerk? What inspired a particular section of your audience might not do the magic with the other section.

Why? Because ***Same conference but different audience . . . or people.*** But one thing remains eternally true: they are all in the conference to benefit, to have access or secret to what you claim to offer from the ads or sales copy you served to the public.

Hence you must keep that expectation high! How? By understanding their mindset! They want to be FREE from the rat race! They want to work less and earn more money! If you have this foreknowledge it would be easy to deliver on your promise, which would be a lot safer for both you and your target audience.

Let's take a practical example. Imagine some of these comedy shows you see around that are being organized almost daily in the country today.

If you're a comedian organizing a show, you should be able to understand the mindset of your participants otherwise you would fail in your profession as a comedian.

As a comedian you should know that one of the reasons your target participants would attend your show is because they want to listen to jokes that would make them laugh their head off, and as such, forget about the pain, disappointment, heartache and stress of daily life without going through the back door.

They want to be free from the shout-down of their selfish, grabby boss; from the practical details of daily activities; from its rules, regulations and limitations.

They just want an atmosphere where they can relax their mind, body and laugh to funny jokes. They are in need of a good humor. And the World out there is not taking it funny with them either.

They want to be free from the envy of friends, family and neighbors. They want the satisfaction of being in the midst of people with the same expectation as theirs! They want the thrill of seeing you doing and saying unusual things from the ones they're already familiar or used to in the World out there! They want to be free from rules and regulations.

So you will make a major mistake if you organize a comedy show and invite a preacher, or start preaching sermons as a comedian. That's a wrong technique (except of course if you're giving a "Christian" joke).

Besides, you're not delivering on your promise. And you can't deliver on your promise once you fail to understand what your participants' wants, once you fail to appeal to their emotion by making them laugh! Hence you must understand their mindset!

Alright, let's look at another example. Imagine you want to organize a speaking event to business executives (i.e. businessmen, managers, CEO, corporate leaders etc).

Your pamphlets or jingles (i.e. ads or sales copy) must project the benefits of attending the seminar to your audience - how to bring more success to their business, because to be successful in their business is their first priority; how to hire employers seeking for job in their organization etc, hence their mindset.

Therefore you must ask yourself: what is their definition of business? And what will business success means to them? How can they attend business success stress-free and without paying much for it?

If you can get to understand their mindset, you will think in line with them, organize you business seminar in anticipation of what they wants!

Getting to Solve Your Money

Now let me tell you a little bit about H2MMS! This is not a theoretical book like the ones you're probably familiar with and that often bore you to death with their non-useful and non do-able information.

With H2MMS! you'll discover the simple secrets to hosting a successful speaking engagement that is related to what you know, have or love doing and that'll bring you more success than you could ever imagine.

H2MMS! shows you how to . . .

1 Organize a speaking conference with just what you know, have or love doing and generate massive income from your speaking engagement.

2 Create a new market niche and style for what you know, have or love doing.

3 Develop your own market strategies towards popularizing and hosting your own speaking event.

The truth is, H2MMS! will help you get into yourself to bring out that latent, dormant, sleeping but **salable ideas** in you that you can use to organize a speaking conference, get audience to attend your conference and generate massive income!

It shows you how to turn words into money with what you have passion and interest for, and how to create a unique image for your seminar rather than simply attending other seminars that cannot produce the most needed response you need to solve your money problem.

In short, you will learn how to become a successful speaker with just what you know, or love doing.

Conclusion

Now that you have read this book on secrets to mastering public speaking and to overcome your fears, certainly you should be able to see that it is not that difficult to face these fears and conquer them.

Let's review how we can conquer the major public speaking fears:

Fear of appearing foolish – forget your past failures, past issues, control your thoughts

Fear of using the wrong words – create new knowledge, develop your vocabulary

Fear of making mistakes – practice, understand communication, prepare your body and mind

Fear of speaking too much – follow the format of introduction, body, conclusion and prepare carefully, time yourself

Fear of being boring – become interesting, read widely to develop confidence, make public speaking a habit.

Once you conquer these five major fears the other fears will dissipate into thin air. In short, to conquer all fears breathe deeply and think critically and creatively!
Read this book as often as you desire, follow its principles, find new ways of developing your mental and speaking skills, until you find yourself becoming the more effective speaker you desire to be

www.ingramcontent.com/pod-product-compliance
Lightning Source LLC
Chambersburg PA
CBHW072014070526
44583CB00015B/1475